Dedicated to Nat Wartels

CLB 1237
© 1985 Illustrations and text: Colour Library Books Ltd.,
    Guildford, Surrey, England.
Display and text filmsetting by Acesetters Ltd.,
    Richmond, Surrey, England.
Produced by AGSA in Barcelona, Spain.
Printed and bound in Barcelona, Spain by Rieusset and Eurobinder.
All rights reserved.
Published 1985 by Crescent Books, distributed by Crown Publishers, Inc.
Printed in Spain
ISBN 0 517 460149
h g f e d c b a

AMERICA
The Fifty States

Text by **Bill Harris**

CRESCENT BOOKS
NEW YORK

CANADA

WASHINGTON
● Olympia

Portland ○

● Salem

OREGON

○ Fort Benton

MONTANA
● Helena

○ Billings

NORTH DAKOTA
● Bismarck

Fargo ○

MINNESOTA

Minneapolis ○
○ St. Paul

WISCONSIN

LAKE SUPERIOR

LAKE MICHIGAN

LAKE HURON

MAINE

● Augusta

Montpelier ●
NEW YORK

VT.

N.H.
● Concord

○ Portland

Boston ●

Boise ●

IDAHO

WYOMING

Cheyenne ●

SOUTH DAKOTA
● Pierre

Madison ●

Milwaukee ●

MICHIGAN

Lansing ●

Detroit ○

LAKE ERIE

Cleveland ○

LAKE ONTARIO

Buffalo ○

Albany ○
Hartford ●

MASS

CONN.

● Providence

R.I.

NEVADA
● Carson City

Sacramento ○

San
Francisco ○

Salt Lake City ●

UTAH

Denver ●

COLORADO

NEBRASKA

Lincoln ●

Omaha ○

IOWA

Des Moines ●

Chicago ○

ILLINOIS

Springfield ●

INDIANA

Indianapolis ●

OHIO

Columbus ●

Cincinnati ○

Pittsburgh ○

PENNSYLVANIA

Harrisburg ●

New York City

N.J.
Trenton ●

WEST VIRGINIA

Washington ○

MD

Annapolis ●

DEL

● Dover

Las ○
Vegas

CALIFORNIA

Los Angeles ○

San Diego ○

ARIZONA

Phoenix ●

Santa Fe ●

Albuquerque ○

NEW MEXICO

Topeka ●

KANSAS

Jefferson City ●

Kansas City ○

St. Louis ○

MISSOURI

Wichita ○

Louisville ○

KENTUCKY

Frankfort ●

Richmond ●

VIRGINIA

Norfolk ○

NORTH CAROLINA

Raleigh ●

Charlotte ○

Tulsa ○

Oklahoma City ●

OKLAHOMA

ARKANSAS

Little Rock ●

Memphis ○

TENNESSEE

Nashville ●

Columbia ●

SOUTH CAROLINA

Charleston ○

Lubbock ○

Dallas ○

Fort Worth ○

El Paso ○

TEXAS

● Austin
Houston ○

San Antonio ○

LOUISIANA

Baton Rouge ●
New Orleans ○

MISSISSIPPI

Jackson ●

Birmingham ○

Montgomery ●

ALABAMA

Atlanta ●

GEORGIA

Tallahassee ●

Jacksonville ○

FLORIDA

Tampa ○

Miami ○

MEXICO

ALASKA

Fairbanks ○

Anchorage ○

GULF OF ALASKA

OAHU

Honolulu ○

MOLOKAI

MAUI

HAWAII

PACIFIC OCEAN

CONTENTS

INTRODUCTION

On July 4, 1776, thirteen English colonies on the Eastern Seaboard of North America declared themselves free, independent and united. The British didn't take that lying down of course, and the thirteen brand-new United States contributed 250,000 men to fight a war that would continue until mid-October, 1781. Of that number 7,000 didn't come back and another 8,500 came home with injuries. But their country was all they hoped it would be and ten years later they added a 14th star to the flag when Vermont was admitted to the Union. By the end of the 18th century two more had been added, Kentucky and Tennessee, and a 61 square-mile tract of land in the center of it all had been declared a Federal District named for the country's first President, George Washington, and designated as its capital.

There were growing pains, to be sure, but as united states, they were able to resolve most of their differences and the accent was on growth and expansion. There was one nagging problem, though, and it came to a head on the day before Christmas in 1860, when South Carolina officially seceded from the Union over the issue of slavery in the South, which they considered an economic necessity and their partners in the North considered an abomination.

It was their contention that though the states had become united under the Constitution, each of them retained many of their own sovereign rights, one of which was to dissolve the partnership. By May, 1861, ten other Southern states had followed the lead and that summer they established a new nation they called the Confederate States of America, with its capital at Richmond, Va. Their official flag, basically red with blue cross bars, contained 13 stars to represent the states involved. Actually there were only 11 states, but factions in Kentucky and Missouri had gone against their governments, both of which had rejected the idea off secession, and had sent delegations to the Confederate Congress.

Maryland and Delaware, two of the original 13 states, voted to stay in the Union and people in the western part of Virginia voted to secede from the state, forming what would later become the independent state of West Virginia.

War was inevitable, of course, and before it was over in 1865, nearly 215,000 Americans had given their lives. When the shooting finally stopped, hostility among the states kept right on raging and the country went through a dozen years of turmoil that ended, uneasily, in 1877 when the new President, Rutherford B. Hayes, removed Federal troops from the South and the country turned its eyes to the West. The year before, Colorado had become 38th of the United States; California and Oregon, as far west as you could go, had already been represented on the American flag for more than two decades. By the close of the 19th century, the number reached 45 when Utah was admitted to the Union. Oklahoma made it 46 in 1907 and Arizona and New Mexico completed the map of the Continental United States in 1912. it was a picture that wouldn't change again until 1959 when both Alaska and Hawaii made America an amalgam of 50 states.

Though the Civil War taught us a valuable lesson about settling domestic differences, there are always differences to be settled. America speaks with a single voice, though the voices you hear as you travel around it are not the same, nor is the countryside. But it's the differences that make it all so interesting. A Virginian looks at life in a slightly different way than a West Virginian, New Yorkers aren't at all like Californians, and you'd better be smiling if you tell a Texan that their wide-open spaces aren't terribly different from the ones of Oklahoma.

And in spite of what you may hear from their neighbors, not one of the 50 states is dull or lifeless or a bad place to live. What follows is a look at some of the individuality, the similarities, the history of each of them.

ALABAMA

Heart of Dixie

Population (1982): 3,943,000 (22nd)

Size: 51,609 square miles (29th)

Entered Union: December 14, 1819 (22nd)

State Motto: We Dare to Defend Our Rights

State Flower: Camellia

State Bird: Yellowhammer

State Tree: Southern pine

Industry: pulp and paper, electronics, textiles, chemicals, shipbuilding

Agriculture: cotton, soybeans, peanuts, pecans, fruit

The history of America is laced with the names of great Spanish, French and English explorers, but Alabama adds one to the lexicon that doesn't quite fit the mold. His name was Prince Modoc, his nationality, Welsh. He sailed into Mobile Bay in 1170 and left his mark all across the state in the form of forts as far north as Tennessee. Four hundred years later, when the Spaniard Alvarez de Pineda arrived and conducted the first Roman Catholic mass in America, he was a little surprised to find that some of the Indians he had come to convert to God had ancestors who spoke Welsh. He was even more surprised to find ruins of forts containing ancient Roman coins and probably never knew that they had been brought there by a Welshman.

Pineda was followed by Cabeza de Vaca, the first Spanish explorer to march to the Pacific Coast, a trip that began in Mobile in 1528, when Alabama was part of Spanish Florida.

When Americans think of the Deep South, Alabama is usually deepest in their thoughts. The Confederate States of America had been formally organized in the State Capitol at Montgomery and the flag of the Confederacy was the flag of preference there well into the 1960s. But if it was the "Cradle of the Confederacy," it was also the "cradle" of the American Civil Rights movement. Martin Luther King, Jr., Ralph Abernathy and Andrew Young all began their careers in Alabama, and place names like Selma and Birmingham are forever linked with their cause.

But if it is perceived as a throwback to the days of slave-owners, the fact is that slave-holding was confined largely to the cotton-producing belt across the south-central part of the state. In the mountains north of Montgomery, the people worked their own farms and, in fact, had come to Alabama from places like Virginia, where an expanding slave economy had forced them off the land.

And the state that calls itself the "Heart of Dixie" is more industrial than the typical vision of Dixieland usually suggests. Birmingham is one of the country's major producers of iron and steel and the basic work on America's arsenal of missiles and rockets was conducted at Huntsville under the direction of Wernher von Braun and his team of German scientists, who took over a plant built to provide material to help fight the Germans in World War II.

But if there are differences among Alabamians, there are similarities, too, and loyalty to each other is one of them. Back in the dark days of Reconstruction after the Civil War, one of the scalawags who tried to take control of one of the counties was unmasked before he succeeded. "We'd have run him out of town," said the editor of the local paper," but he was from around here."

Previous page: the Parker Ranch, Hawaii. Facing page: Alabama's State Capitol, Montgomery. Overleaf: Gaineswood in Demopolis.

Above: Gaineswood in Demopolis, one of the finest Greek Revival houses in the South. For eight years Mobile was the capital of French Colonial America and the elegance of this early influence can still be found in Oakleigh (facing page), a home of the 1830s.

ALASKA

Population (1982): 438,000 (50th)

Size: 586,412 square miles (1st)

Entered Union: January 3, 1959 (49th)

State Motto: North to The Future

State Flower: Forget-me-not

State Bird: Willow ptarmigan

State Tree: Sitka spruce

Industry: oil, tourism, fishing, lumber

Agriculture: barley, potatoes, hay, dairy products

It's entirely appropriate that Alaska was one of the last two states admitted to the Union. More than any other it is still a place where a family can lead a life similar to the pioneers who expanded the country westward. And more than any other, there is more future there than past.

Almost 90 percent of the 438,000 people who live in its nearly 587,000 square miles either came from one of the other states or have parents who did, but few have any intention of going back. By and large they like it there, where the wilderness is at your back door and the idea of "rugged individualism" is a necessary way of life.

It's a place of spectacular scenery that includes North America's highest mountain, its biggest glaciers, the greatest untouched wilderness anywhere in the United States.

It's a place that was largely left untouched by the government after it was bought from Russia for $7.2 million in 1867. It wasn't until 1903 that a Congressional committee was formed to have a legislative look at the place, and their findings didn't go far beyond the discovery that there wasn't a single road a wagon could use anywhere in the territory. It took them ten more years to do anything about it and then all they did was build a 370-mile dirt road from Valdez on the coast to Fairbanks in the interior.

Things got better during World War II, when the territory was considered strategic and roads vital to the war effort, but the government went to sleep again until the late 1950s when Alaska was grudgingly included in the Federal Highway Program. The result is that the roads in Alaska aren't as good or as extensive as in any other state. The result of that is that most Alaskans live in communities, but not many of their towns are connected together. Except by air. Alaskans use airplanes almost as much as their fellow Americans use automobiles. It's the only way to get around the vast territory, they say. But just as important, the freedom of flight appeals to their pioneering spirit, the same spirit that sets them apart from their neighbors to the south.

Because a huge part of the state lies north of the Arctic Circle and because it is a land dotted with glaciers and snow-capped mountains, most Americans think of Alaska as a place where you never shed your woollies. The fact is that along the Pacific coast, the climate is very much like New England, except the winters are a bit warmer. Up in the Yukon, the territory Jack London told us about, the winter temperatures drop 40 or 50 degrees below zero Fahrenheit, but as any sourdough up in Nome will tell you, there is no wind. And it could be worse. Fort Yukon has recorded temperatures as low as 78 degrees below zero in January. That same year, the mercury went up to 100 in June.

Facing page: a distant view of Mount Kimble in the Alaska Range. Overleaf: (left) a typical small Alaskan port and (right) Mineral Creek, near Valdez.

ARIZONA

Grand Canyon State

Population (1982): 2,860,000 (29th)

Size: 113,309 square miles (6th)

Entered Union: February 14, 1912 (48th)

State Motto: Ditat Deus (God Enriches)

State Flower: Saguaro cactus

State Bird: Cactus wren

State Tree: Paloverde

Industry: electronics, printing, clothing, aircraft

Agriculture: cotton, corn, sugar beets, citrus fruits

Before the 1950s, Arizona was a classic example of a nice place to visit, but not so terrific as a place to live. What made the difference between then and now was air conditioning. This is a place where it almost never rains and the sun beats down without mercy. But that's why it's so beautiful and why more than two billion years of geological history is so dazzlingly displayed in the Grand Canyon, the Painted Desert, Monument Valley and the Petrified Forest.

After the air conditioners made it possible to live there comfortably, Arizona got a reputation as a perfect place for retirement and with it, a perception among other Americans that it was a place populated by old folks. The fact is that the median age is under 30 and the state has one of the highest birth rates in the country.

It took more than air conditioning to accomplish that. In 1911, when Arizona was not yet a state, the Federal Government built a dam on the Salt River to irrigate the land in the Phoenix area, creating an oasis that's home to more than half the state's population. Other dams and water projects, including Hoover Dam and Glen Canyon Dam, have given them the water they need to grow and the power that runs the industries that lure as many people there in search of jobs as for the good life in the sun.

A Government explorer once told his employers in Washington that Arizona was completely without value. He was wrong, of course, but that's one reason why 13 different tribes of Indians live there today. More than a quarter of the state is devoted to Indian reservations, possibly because Government officials believed what their explorer told them. They were big on giving the most valueless acres to Indians. But in this case, they were wrong. There is coal under some of that land, and there are white men eager to get at it. But in the 20th century, unlike the 19th when the reservations simply would have been moved, it's up to the tribal councils to decide and, with a few exceptions, the decisions have been to leave things the way they were. And that seems fitting because, as anyone who lives there will tell you proudly, Arizona is the place "where time stands still."

But that's only partly true. Phoenix is 20 times bigger today than it was in 1950, and though still smaller and more faithful to its original Spanish roots, Tucson is growing at almost the same rate.

And why not? It's a terrific place to live. If you have an air conditioner.

Facing page: London Bridge at Lake Havasu City on the Colorado River. Overleaf: (left) Tucson and (right) Tombstone.

Phoenix (facing page) gained its name from the fact that it rose near the site of a long-dead Indian settlement. The State Capitol (above) in Phoenix is built of local tufa and granite. Overleaf: Canyon de Chelly (left) contains evidence of five Indian cultures. Montezuma Castle National Monument (right) stands in the Verde River Valley.

The forces of erosion have sculpted Arizona into some of the most spectacular scenery in America. Facing page: the
Grand Canyon, which is more than a mile in depth and is cut by the Colorado River, (above) Monument Valley,
(overleaf, left) the Colorado at Lipan Point and (overleaf, right) the Grand Canyon at Yaki Point.

ARKANSAS

Land of Opportunity

Population (1982): 2,291,000 (33rd)

Size: 53,104 square miles (27th)

Entered Union: June 15, 1836 (25th)

State Motto: Regnat Populus (The People Rule)

State Flower: Apple blossom

State Bird: Mockingbird

State Tree: Pine

Industry: poultry, forest products, aluminum, clothing, electrical products

Agriculture: soybeans, rice, cotton, wheat

If William Shakespeare were to come back to life, the one place in America where he'd be comfortable with the English language would be in the Ozark Mountains of Arkansas. But that fact has been responsible for generations of Americans regarding Arkies as illiterate hillbillies who talk funny, sip moonshine from Mason jars, and whose women wear hightop shoes and poke bonnets. It's true that a genuine Ozark accent isn't like anything else in the English-speaking world. If you don't feel well, they say you're "dauncy" and if you have a raffle, you'd better be careful not to shoot anyone with it.

The speech patterns are Elizabethan, brought from England with the original settlers and preserved over the years by the isolation of the rugged mountains.

The "Lil' Abner" image was finally put to rest in 1966 when they elected no less a person than Winthrop Rockefeller to be their Governor. He brought industry to the state and upgraded its educational system, but more important, he made Americans in other states realize that Arkansas was ready to join the American mainstream.

The Ozark plateau accounts for only a quarter of the state's geography, even though it had for all those years accounted for 90 percent of its image. The Mississippi River is its eastern border, and its Delta farmland is as representative of the Old South as any place can be. In the southern part of the state, swamps and pine forests reinforce the image. But the War Between the States had little impact on Arkansas. Most of its people weren't involved in a slave-oriented economy and the mountains kept them isolated from any sympathy with the Northern cause.

In the southwestern part of the state, cattle ranches and oil rigs give it a Wild West flavor. And in the center, along the navigable Arkansas River, cities like Little Rock and Fort Smith have become bustling ports.

Up in the hills, folks are tired of the opinions of people from other places; opinions which to them were often "worse than smellin' whiskey through a jailhouse winder." But they're still not rushing headlong into the 20th century. Life isn't bad up there, in spite of what other folks say. And proof of that may well be the reason why the Ozarks are experiencing a population growth spearheaded by retirees who find the countryside beautiful and the people pleasant to have as neighbors. Even if they do talk funny.

Facing page: Arkansas' State Capitol in Little Rock. Overleaf: (left) the Capitol and Little Rock at dusk, and (right) the Old State House in Little Rock, state capitol from 1833 until 1911.

CALIFORNIA

Golden State

Population (1982): 24,724,000 (1st)

Size: 158,693 square miles (3rd)

Entered Union: September 9, 1850 (31st)

State Motto: Eureka (I Have Found It)

State Flower: Golden poppy

State Bird: California valley quail

State Tree: California redwood

Industry: electronic equipment, aerospace, machinery, chemicals recreation

Agriculture: cotton, vegetables, grapes and wine, fruits, dairy products

In the 1950s, John Gunther said that of all the states, California was the only one that could be a country all by itself. A lot of Americans think it already is. "They're not like us," many people say. "They have developed a culture all their own." It's not quite true. What they probably have developed is an intensification of the American culture. It's only natural. Most Californians come from other parts of America and they went west looking for improvement.

In the 1960s, when California passed New York as the most populous state, new residents were pouring in at the incredible rate of over a thousand a day. By 1982, it was ahead of New York by almost 8 million people, the entire population of New York City.

In Los Angeles, California has the city most Americans love to dislike and in San Francisco, the one more single out as their favorite. There are a lot of things other Americans envy about Californians. The fact that they own half the swimming pools in the country and that more pleasure boats are in California water than in any other state are only part of it. They buy more cars, are more likely to sleep in a waterbed, or at least a king-size bed, and more of them own vacation homes than any other group of Americans.

They drink more (except for their neighbors in Nevada) and they use more drugs than people in any other state. But they seem to enjoy themselves in other ways, too. They lead the nation in ownership of campers and dune buggies and surfboards.

And if they seem to be just living for today, survey after survey reveals that Californians, more than most Americans, are high on the future. They think, if anything, their lives are getting better. And they may be right.

They surely have a beautiful setting for it. From the beautiful Yosemite Valley to the spectacular Mojave Desert to the redwood forests, the vineyard country and the wild coast of the Pacific, few states have such variety of natural beauty.

But was John Gunther right? Could California become a world power in her own right? It's already bigger than all but about 100 of the world's countries and not many more than that in terms of population. It produces more than all but six, including the United States of course, and its per capita income is greater than any country in the world, also including the United States.

But there are no plans in Sacremento to make the Golden State a golden country, which makes a lot of people in Washington sleep a lot easier.

Facing page: California's Capitol in Sacramento. Overleaf: (left) Pacific Palisades, Los Angeles and (right) Hotel del Coronado on San Diego Bay.

Facing page: the sailing ship *Star of India* rests in San Diego Harbor beneath the modern buildings. Above: a Greek temple imported from Europe and a Classical-style pool in the grounds of William Randolph Hearst's fabulous palace at San Simeon. Overleaf: (left) the Pacific Palisades, Los Angeles. (Right) the liner *Queen Mary*, now a floating hotel and museum berthed at Long Beach.

Above: an aerial view of the luxury, 300-room Beverly Hills Hotel. Los Angeles' magnificent Memorial Coliseum (facing page) was enlarged in 1932 to host the 10th Olympiad. Overleaf: (left) Universal Studios, Hollywood, where visitors are taken on conducted tours of movie sets. (Right) the J. Paul Getty Museum in Malibu, built in the style of an ancient Roman villa.

Above: the famous Hollywood Bowl which occupies a natural amphitheater in the hills.
Facing page: Los Angeles from the southwest. Overleaf: (left) Pinnacle Cove in Point
Lobos State Reserve. (Right) the dramatically-sited Cypress Point Golf Course.

Above: a view from Cypress Point on the Monterey Peninsula. Along the coast, on Highway 1, is Bixby Creek Bridge (facing page) which arches gracefully 260 feet above the stream. Overleaf: (left) Grant Avenue in San Francisco's Chinatown area and (right) the very steep, and winding, Lombard Street in San Francisco.

San Francisco: (previous pages, left and overleaf, right) the magnificent Golden Gate Bridge, (previous pages, right) gingerbread houses, (above) Grant Avenue, the narrow but bustling thoroughfare which bisects Chinatown from north to south, (facing page) Fisherman's Wharf, an area of fish restaurants and souvenir shops and (overleaf, left) the Oakland Bay Bridge.

COLORADO

Centennial State

Population (1982): 3,045,000 (27th)

Size: 104,247 square miles (8th)

Entered Union: August 1, 1876 (38th)

State Motto: Nil Sine Numine (Nothing Without Providence)

State Flower: Rocky Mountain columbine

State Bird: Lark bunting

State Tree: Colorado blue spruce

Industry: electronics and computers, aerospace, minerals, steel

Agriculture: corn, wheat, hay, sugar beets, fruit

Ask anyone how much of the land area of Colorado is in the Rocky Mountains and the answer will very likely be "all of it." Half of it is closer to the truth, but Colorado's heart is in the mountains and more than 80 percent of the state's population lives at the edge of the Rockies in a belt that stretches from Fort Collins in the north to Colorado Springs in the south.

At the center of it all is Denver, world-famous as the "mile-high city," but even it isn't as much in the mountains as at their feet, on the outside looking up.

There are more than two dozen multi-million dollar ski resorts in Colorado, mostly on the western side of the mountains, including Vail, a 1960s idea of a quaint Alpine village, and Aspen, a former silver-mining town that was turned into a gold mine of a resort in the early 1950s. With more than 200 miles of ski trails and 30 lifts, it is overwhelmingly the biggest ski resort in the United States.

The mountains are what lured most Colorado families there, and they are what keep their children there, which is why, until the population boom in the years after World War II, the state boasted more citizens born within its borders than any other in the West. "Where can you go that's more beautiful?" they ask. In all of North America there are 81 mountain peaks rising to more than 14,000 feet and 54 of them are in Colorado, and there are no other peaks in all of the Rocky Mountains higher than any of them.

But what about the other half? The eastern part of the state is part of the Great Plains, where irrigation makes it possible for huge mechanized farms to produce respectable crops of beets, corn and grain. South and west of Pueblo, the population is largely of Spanish descent, some of whom can trace their ancestry back to the first settlers who moved into the San Luis Valley with the Spanish Conquistadores when the territory was an undisputed part of Mexico. Irrigation keeps the valley lush as it does out on the Plains, but the good life enjoyed among their neighbors along the eastern slopes of the mountains is elusive to them.

The result is that population in southern Colorado is dropping. It's dropping in the eastern part of the state, too, where mechanization has made farms bigger and manpower needs smaller. But through it all, the population of Colorado is growing at a faster rate than that of almost any other state in the Union. It has more than doubled in the past 40 years.

Blame the mountains. Just as in the days when pioneers hung banners from the sides of their wagons saying "Pikes Peak or Bust," and then headed for Colorado Springs, the Rockies never fail to overwhelm a visitor. To many, they are a barrier against going any further west, to most they are a lure that make it hard to contemplate ever going back east.

Facing page: the State Capitol in Denver. Overleaf: (left) Denver's Civic Center and (right) the business district.

The "Mile High City" of Denver (above) is important, not for its altitude, but for its financial and transportation facilities. Facing page: Court Place Plaza, Denver. Overleaf: (left) the Great Sand Dunes National Monument beneath the Sangre de Cristo Range. (Right) part of the aspen forests so typical of the state.

cing page: the jagged peaks of the Maroon Bells rise majestically above the rippling waters of Maroon Lake.
aroon Creek (above) snakes away towards Aspen before meeting the Roaring Fork River. Overleaf: (left) the
immering waters of Dream Lake. (Right) aspens and conifers at Independence Pass.

CONNECTICUT

Nutmeg State

Population (1982): 3,153,000 (26th)

Size: 5,009 square miles (48th)

Entered Union: January 9, 1788 (5th)

State Motto: Qui Transtulit Sustinet (He Who is Transplanted Still Sustains)

State Flower: Mountain laurel

State Bird: Robin

State Tree: White oak

Industry: aircraft engines, submarines, helicopters, copper products,
machine tools

Agriculture: tobacco, hay, apples, nursery stock

Anyone trying to convey a sense of small-town America can do it by calling the small town "Podunk." Though there is no such town, the name was given to a tribe of Indians living in the beautiful Connecticut River Valley in 1614 by the Dutch explorer Adriaen Block, the first European to visit there. By the time English settlers arrived from the Massachusetts colony 20 years later, the Dutch already had a tenuous claim on the place and an outpost of New Amsterdam on the site of what is now Hartford.

The tension between the two groups gave the American English language another pair of words. The Dutch were outnumbered and frightened to the point of building a wall at the north end of their colony, on Manhattan Island, to keep the English out. The site is known everywhere in the world today as Wall Street. But wall or no, the Dutch knew in their hearts that it was only a matter of time before their Connecticut neighbors would overrun them and they covered their fears with a bravado that, to them at least, passed for wit. The English were known as "John Bull" even then, and Peter Stuyvesant's followers thought it was great fun to mock them as "John Cheese" whenever they had an encounter. In their language, John Cheese is "Jon Quese," which to British ears came out as "Yankee," a word Connecticut people used all over New England to describe themselves.

Nearness to New York has always loomed large in the development of Connecticut. Though never really great farming country, the hills and valleys, the northern coast of Long Island Sound, are strikingly beautiful and almost from the beginning wealthy New Yorkers were lured there in search of a house in the country.

The result, in part at least, is that though Connecticut is one of the smallest of the states, its per-capita income is one of the highest. It has become corporate headquarters to some of America's biggest companies, too, and its rolling hills are as much dotted with stainless steel and glass as with the quaint stone walls that have been a Connecticut institution since the earliest days.

After Yale University settled down in New Haven in 1716, the state became a haven for education and Connecticut is home to many of the best prep schools in the country, where future Ivy Leaguers get a head start not only on their education, but on their social contacts as well.

Before the Revolution, England's government placed restrictions on the amount of manufacturing that could be done in Connecticut. The Connecticut Yankees got even during the war, when they became the new country's biggest producer of arms and ammunition. Samuel Colt, inventor of the "gun that won the West," started his career in Hartford; the Winchester company in New Haven provided the long rifles. And that may be one reason why Hartford has been America's insurance capital for generations.

Facing page: the State Capitol in Hartford. Overleaf: (left) Yale University in New Haven. (Right) Mystic, home of the fastest clipper ships of the nineteenth century.

Mystic Seaport (these pages) is a beautiful recreation of this
great 19th-century ship-building town, complete with ships,
buildings and craftsmen from across the state.

DELAWARE

Diamond State

Population (1982): 602,000 (47th)

Size: 2,057 square miles (49th)

Entered Union: December 7, 1787 (1st)

State Motto: Liberty and Independence

State Flower: Peach blossom

State Bird: Blue hen chicken

State Tree: Holly

Industry: synthetic fibers, processed foods, railroad equipment, automobiles

Agriculture: soybeans, corn, mushrooms, vegetables

It was the first to call itself a state and first to ratify the Constitution that created the United States. It had been a Dutch colony and a Swedish colony, part of William Penn's Royal grant that established Pennsylvania and at the same time part of the King's gift to Lord Baltimore that established Maryland. But none of that is as important to the history of Delaware as what happened in 1802, when a young man looked at dozens of sites between New York and Washington and almost indifferently settled on a spot along the Brandywine Creek a few miles north of Wilmington.

His name was Eleuthere Irenee Du Pont. The site he picked was for a gunpowder plant. By the time the Civil war broke out, his company was producing more than half the gunpowder in the United States, and wars in the United States and Europe made the Du Pont descendants, not to mention Delaware itself, very wealthy indeed.

The company hasn't made a stick of dynamite since 1974, but innovations in other fields of chemistry, and products such as Dacron and Orlon, Lucite and Mylar have given it a reputation for innovation that make Du Pont one of the biggest family-owned companies in the world.

If it's a big company, it's a big family, too, and many of its members have been part of the state's government for generations. All that has been good for Delaware. Some years ago, when he was frustrated by the legislature's lack of activity in funding new schools, a man named Du Pont built them with his own money. Another personally paid for the construction of the state's first paved road.

But Du Pont benevolence doesn't tell the whole story of why personal taxes are so low and services so good for the average Delawarean. About a third of the corporations listed on the two major American stock exchanges are incorporated in Delaware, upwards of 80,000 of them. That's not to say that 80,000 Chairmen-of-The-Boards pull into Wilmington in their limousines every morning. In fact, few have probably ever been to Delaware at all. But the papers that make their companies legal entities are filed in row after row of cabinets in Dover, the state capital. And once a year, each of them gets a receipt for state taxes added to the file. To be sure, they are just about the lowest state corporate taxes in the country, but it does add up, after all.

It's especially incredible when you think what it all cost in the first place. Peter Minuit, whose place in history was assured when he bought the Island of Manhattan from the Indians for $24, did even better here. He bought all the territory along the Delaware River watershed for a single copper pot.

Facing page: the Townsend Building in Dover.

Facing page: the Capitol Building, Dover, is one of the nation's oldest
capitols still in use. Above: Rehoboth Beach. Overleaf: (left) a farm near
Farmington. (Right) a stablehand at work in the Moore Stables.

DISTRICT OF COLUMBIA

Population (1982): 631,000

Size: 67 square miles

Motto: Justita Omnibus (Justice for All)

Flower: American beauty rose

Bird: Wood thrush

Tree: Scarlet oak

Industry: Politics and government

Washington, D.C. isn't like most of the other capitals of major countries. It isn't like other American cities, either. It was planned that way.

The District of Columbia was established by an act of Congress in 1790 which authorized the President to select a site "not exceeding ten miles square" in the region of the Potomac River. The site was a compromise between factions representing the Northern and Southern states, but the location, though central at the time, is more Southern than Northern.

The so-called Federal Town, President Washington decided, would be on the banks of the river in territory mostly in Maryland, but partly in Virginia. By the time he picked the site, he had also picked a town planner and designer, Pierre Charles L'Enfant. Together they approached the local landowners and secured an agreement that the territory would be sold to the Government for $66.66 an acre for land that would be used for public buildings. The remainder would be divided into building lots they could sell themselves, though the proceeds from every second sale would go to the Government to develop the city. Another part of the agreement said that land for highways and streets would be turned over to the Government at no cost. That's when the trouble began. L'Enfant's plan called for streets 110 feet wide and avenues 160 feet wide. Then he added insult to injury with a proposed avenue 400 feet wide and a mile long.

Washington supported him in the face of withering fire from his neighbors along the Potomac. The plan was accepted, the deeds signed. But before work actually began, a landowner built a house that blotted out one of the planner's vistas. L'Enfant asked that it be torn down and when he got a refusal, he tore it down himself. He got fired for his trouble. He was offered $2500 for the work he had done, plus a choice building lot near the President's Mansion. He turned down both and eventually died a broken man.

But his dream was realized. The city, encompassing nearly 70 square miles, grew according to his plan, resulting in an unusually beautiful city by any standard, which has become one of the country's most pleasant places to live. That's one reason why so many people work so hard for the privilege.

Because it was established as a capital city and not as a state, people who live there didn't have the right to vote until 1964, when they won the right to have a say in presidential elections. It wasn't until ten years later that they were able to choose members of their city government and even now, though they have one representative in the House of Representatives, that person may not vote on the House floor, but may participate in committees. They have no representative in the Senate, though Congress has the power to veto actions by its 13-member city council and has complete control over the city's budget.

Facing page: the Federal Capitol on Capitol Hill. Overleaf: (left) the original buildings of the Smithsonian Institution. (Right) the 555-foot-tall Washington Monument.

Previous pages: (left) the White House, home of presidents, and (right) the Lincoln Memorial, with each column representing on of the states at the time of his death. Above: Arlington National Cemetery. Facing page: the Vietnam Veterans Memorial. The Jefferson Memorial (overleaf, left) contains a 19-foot statue of Thomas Jefferson. Overleaf: (right) the Washington monument.

ROBERT D MERRELL • GEORGE A MORGAN •
ALLEN L PIERCE • DONALD C PIPER • WILLIE PIPPINS Sr •
BENNIE LEE SIMMONS • FREDERICK A SLEMP • CECIL Y WARE •
TOMMIE LEE WILLIAMS • JESSE J BOLTON • FRANKLIN V BRODNIK •
NICHOLES SOCHACKI • JAMES M TERMINI • CLYDE W WITHEE •
SIMMIE BELLAMY Jr • ELMER E BERRY • THOMAS C BREWER Jr •
IRVIN CLARKE Jr • CHARLIES E DANIELS • JOHNSON F FRANK •
JACK L HIMES • ROBERT L HOSKINS Jr • DANIEL R JAMES •
DONALD S NEWTON • ROBERT D WILLIAMS Jr • FREDERICK E SMITH •
BILLIE N PLUM • FRANCIS D WILLS • WILLIAM F AYRES •
PAUL E HELSEL Jr • RICK E KOPKA • LAWRENCE B McCLOUD •
JAMES M SPENCE • ROGER D BULIFANT • HENRY C CASEBOLT •
CLEGG • PETER W FIELDS • WILLIAM FUCHS Jr • FRANKLIN D R GILBERT •
ARTHUR J JACKSON • MARSHALL JESSIE • CHARLES JOHNSON •
LAIRD • RAYMOND E MEYERS • KENNETH D MIDDLETON • MARK L MORGAN •
McCARTHY • BRENT A McCLELLAN • GEORGE F McCOY • CURTIS J McGEE •
JAMES R McLEMORE • JOSE TORRES • RICHARD J WOLCHESKI •
PEDERSON • MICHAEL D PLISKA • DARRELL T RAY • ALBERT C ROBERTS •
ROGERS • CHARLES W SIMS • CLIFTON L TART • MIGUEL E NARANJO Jr •
F NUGENT • CLARK N WOODWORTH Jr • CHARLIE M YOUNG •
CHRISTENSEN • WILLIAM P FORAN • WILLIAM D FRAWLEY • ALBERT F BAIRD •
JOHN W WILLIAMS • DONALD J WOLOST • DONALD P KING •
HATCHER • MARSHALL M HOLT Jr • JACK M HO • BOBLISH •
CHARLES F COINER • ROBERT F FIELDER • JENKINS •
P ALSTED • CHARLES W RADER • DENNIS L • GREENE •
III • STUART M ANDREWS • HERIBERTO ARMENTA • GARY C ALLEN •
DANIEL P BIRCH • RAYMOND BLANCHETTE • JAMES S COCCHIARA •
BUSH • RUPERT S CARVEN III • PHILLIP H CLARK • WILLIAM W BROWN •
CORSON • BRUCE DAVIS • STANLEY T DEMBOSKI • LESTER R ATHERDEN •
GARNETT Jr • ANDREW L HASTINGS • RONALD W GODDARD • SEAN P DODSON •
DAVID M HANN • JOHN M HARDEN • HARRY M GODWIN •
HERRON • JOHNNY RAY HOLLOWAY • MICHAEL A GILSON • HARRY P HELT Jr •
JOHNSON • HARVEY W JONES • HENRY J HOOPER • WILLIAM J HRINKO •
KOLBECK • ROBERT B LABBE • ARNELL KEYES • LEWIS A KIMMEL Jr •
R LYDEN • DIEGO MERCADO • JACK W LINDSEY • FRANK LOPEZ Jr •
ORLANDO • PAUL G PARSONS • VINFORD F MICHAEL • PETER G SCAVUZZO •
McMILLIN • JAMES R SCOTT • JACKIE D REYNOLDS • JOSEPH R REYNOLDS •
BELL • DELBERT L TRUBE Jr • MICHAEL A SHANDS • ALFRED J SMITH •
LEWIS D BELL • RAY MAX BARNWELL • ROSCOE L VICK • CHARLES D WADSWORTH •
ALBERT CABANYAN • MANCHINI • CHARLES R WETZEL • MICHAEL R YOUNG •
DOSTER • JAMES H EDGE • MALLENDA CALIBOSO • JAMES J BRADLEY • KENNETH A SMITH • WILLIE JOE BRAMLET •
GONZALES • JOSEPH C EVANS Jr • CHARLES L EDWARDS • PHILIP FITCH • ROBERT C HESSOM •
FORD • ROY L HARRISON • FRED M HORTON • THOMAS A JENNINGS • ROBERT C LYNCH •
LYDEN • THOMAS D McCLEEN • STEVEN A CHURCH • THOMAS W EDWARDS •
JOSE A LAGUER • LOUIS P HERNANDEZ • RICKEY D GARNER • CHARLES E CRUTCHFIELD •
SETZER • CHESTER L OWENS • DENNIS A McGEE • AUGUSTUS A HULTQUIST •
NIXON • JOEL A BOWDEN • JOSE L JIMENEZ • MARIO C KITTS • THOMAS A •
GLEZ • DAVID A STOUT • DANNY A SMITH • TOMMY R MILLER •
JAMES ALEXANDER • CLYDE M HALL •

JAMES L TEWKSBURY • CURTIS E •
DAVID M DAVIES • DONALD R BU •
WILLIAM D HASTY • JAMES MOOR •
NORMAN N MILLER • PAUL R HATT •
THURMAN W OWEN • DANIEL J PI •
KEITH L SHIPP • JIMMY B TAYLOR •
RALPH M WILLIAMS • RICHARD H •
GARY D NAIL • DAVID E HORNBY •
ARTHUR C MORRIS Jr • KENNETH D •
DONOVAN J PRUETT • TOMMIE LEE •
JACK D GILBERT • FRANKLIN E HOSLE •
JAMES W BROWN • GERMAN CHAPA •
KEITH W KAUFFMAN • HAROLD W LO •
LAWRENCE McCREA • CHARLIE REED •
EDWARD M STANCHEK • FRANKLIN F •
ARNOLD WOODSON • BERNARD BA •
DENNIS P COOK • JAMES W GATES •
ROBERT A KREUZIGER • JOHN W LAFAY •
THOMAS J RALSTON • JACK A SMITH •
JOHN M BROWN III • MARTIN COX • W •
ARTHUR J BAYLOR • THOMAS T WALKER •
GEORGE L SAMUELS • CHARLES M SHEL •
RALPH S KOROLZYK • THOMAS W MUIR •
RONALD T SHELTON • TOM K TINGLE • LU •
HOWARD C BLEVINS • RICHARD F BUBA •
RALPH COLEMAN • ZED C CREVELING •
JOHN H EAGLIN • PHILYAW FEE • EUGENE •
DONALD W HALL • DAVID A HAMMETT •
PHILIP A JONES • EVERETT E LANGSTON •
RICHARD NOYOLA • JAMES W ROBINSON •
EDWARD W REILLY • CHARLES D OGLESBY •
J C LESLIE SHORT • JOSEPH F SMITH • THO •
GEORGE H WARD • JOHN A WATKINS •
LAVALL DURR • WILLIAM A GLASSON • ERIC •
EDMUND H HORNSTEIN • RONNIE RAY LO •
COLEY L WASHINGTON • FRED A BENNER •
JESSE L CLARK II • GREEN CONLEY •
LLOYD FIELDS Jr • PHILLIPS LAMARR •
JOSE A PACHECO • FRANK A •
JOHN C MAPE • RONALD G SOULE • RICHA •
CHARLES J MURPHY • JIMMY RAY WOLFE •
LEWIS M THOMAS Jr • BURTON A •
RALPH H LIVESAY • ROBERT I •
WALTER HA •

FLORIDA

Sunshine State

Population (1982): 10,416,000 (7th)

Size: 58,560 square miles (22nd)

Entered Union: March 3, 1845 (27th)

State Motto: In God We Trust

State Flower: Orange blossom

State Bird: Mockingbird

State Tree: Sabal palmetto palm

Industry: electronics, tourism, printing, textiles

Agriculture: citrus fruits, vegetables, sugarcane, tobacco, watermelons

At the last official count, there were 10,416,000 people living in Florida, and not one of them lives more than 75 miles from either the Atlantic Ocean or the Gulf of Mexico. But if they don't want to travel that far, the state also has 30,000 lakes, most of which are great for boating, water skiing and fishing. It's true that a lot of other states have a lot of water, but few have as much sun to go with it. The sun has been behind everything, from the state's population growth from less than two million before World War II, to the industries that keep them employed.

Florida grows more citrus than any other state and only California produces more fresh vegetables for winter consumption. It's also home to cattle ranches, sugar plantations and pine woods that feed a respectable paper industry. But the biggest industry of all is tourism, luring more that 35 million people a year to play in the sun and splash in the water.

Florida's 2,276 miles of seacoast take it further south than any other point in the United States; its northernmost point is further south than the lower end of California. But none of Florida is below the Tropic of Cancer, which makes the climate more variable, and often more bearable, than in the tropics.

It first attracted the attention of the Spanish in 1513, when the Governor of Puerto Rico, Ponce de Leon, heard there was a fountain of youth over there and went to Florida to find it. Almost as if the search is continuing, the state seems most attractive to older people and more than a quarter of the population is over 55. But there are enough young people there to put the lie to the story that Florida is the Retirement State.

The Spanish stayed in Florida for more that 300 years, but not much happened while they were there except they were successful in keeping the French and the English out. Not much happened after the Americans took over, either. They fought bloody wars with the Indians and participated half-heartedly in the Civil War. In the years before, it had been the focal point of the Spanish Main, with pirates roaming up and down the Gulf Coast and the Indian population less than friendly. The American population that moved in after the Spanish moved out in 1821 were mainly from other Southern States, most often Georgia, which contributed men who strutted their authority behind cracking bull whips, giving the nickname "cracker" to native Floridians.

Plush resorts and new rail links with the North that were established in the 1880s finally put Florida on the map and the trend has been upward ever since. In the years after the First World War, when servicemen had discovered the Florida climate while in training there, the state experienced the biggest real estate boom any state has ever seen. They even sold land that was underwater, which makes it hard to believe there is any left. But there is, and the boom continues.

Facing page: Tallahassee, state capital of Florida. Overleaf: (left) Daytona Beach. (Right) a marina in Downtown Miami.

Previous pages: (left) a liner leaving Miami Harbor, and (right) the John F. Kennedy Space Center on Cape Canaveral. Above: Miami at night. Jacksonville (facing page) is a major port and trading city. Overleaf: (left) cypress trees near Winter Haven, a scene typical of inland Florida. (Right) sunset at Whale Harbor.

GEORGIA

Peach State

Population (1982): 5,639,000 (12th)

Size: 58,876 square miles (21st)

Entered Union: January 2, 1788 (4th)

State Motto: Wisdom, Justice and Moderation

State Flower: Cherokee rose

State Bird: Brown thrasher

State Tree: Live oak

Industry: textiles, clothing, wood products, chemical products

Agriculture: peanuts, corn, soybeans, tobacco, cotton

For generations, the standard joke among Southern farmers was that when they died, they didn't know whether they were headed for Heaven or Hell, but they knew for sure that they'd have to change trains at Atlanta. Even then, though it was the crossroads of the American South, Atlanta was probably the least Southern of all Southern cities.

Today it presents even less of the traditional Southern image and the joke about changing trains has become intensified, though it's not trains any longer, but airplanes. Atlanta's airport is the biggest and busiest in the South and almost nobody goes anywhere south of Washington, D.C. without at least touching down there. The city itself looks like a place on the move, with gleaming skyscrapers often connected to one another by futuristic bridges high above street level.

But if Atlanta has shed its sleepy Southern image, the rest of the state, though far from sleepy, has kept in touch with the past. Savannah, especially, after years of neglect, has been restoring its old houses and commercial buildings to create one of the most charming cities anywhere in America. And all over the state, small towns still have a turn-of-the-century character and people still spend quiet summer evenings sitting on the front porch, just as they've done for years. After church on Sunday, the generations mix as families get together for hearty Sunday dinners, a tradition in many parts of America, but almost a fine art in Georgia.

Georgia is well-known to most Americans as a producer of cotton and peaches, but the Georgia product they know best isn't always associated with the state. Back in 1886, John Pemberton, an Atlanta pharmacist, had an idea for a new patent medicine that would cure hangovers. He mixed the ingredients in an old cast-iron pot in his backyard, and though history doesn't record whether he had a hangover at the time, he liked the way it tasted and promptly mixed another batch. Now, old John was a tinkerer, not a businessman and he was pleased when another pharmacist named Asa Griggs Candler paid him $2300 for the formula. It was a lot of money in those days and it left Pemberton free to concoct some other patent medicines, maybe even a better hangover cure.

On the other hand, when he retired in 1916, Candler was worth $50 million. The formula he bought was for a drink they called Coca-Cola. The company he built is worth some $2 billion today. So much for the sleepy Southern image.

The elegant, columned Capitol (facing page) graces Atlanta.
Overleaf: (left) Downtown Atlanta and (right) Hurt Park.

Jekyll Island, off the Georgia coast, was once the pleasure ground of millionaires, and some of their "cottages" (these pages) remain. Overleaf: (left) elegant Hay House in Macon. (Right) Fort McAllister, the southernmost fortification defending Savannah's coast, resisted numerous attacks until it fell on December 13, 1864.

HAWAII

Aloha State

Population (1982): 994,000 (39th)

Size: 6,450 square miles (47th)

Entered Union: August 21, 1959 (50th)

State Motto: The Life of The Land is Perpetuated in Righteousness

State Flower: Hibiscus

State Bird: Hawaiian goose

State Tree: Candlenut

Industry: sugar, canning, clothing, tourism

Agriculture: sugar, pineapples, fruits, coffee, vegetables

It's more than 2400 miles from the American continent and a huge proportion of its population has come from the Asian continent. Its landscapes include volcanoes and rain forests, and the people work at keeping the native language alive as well as the old customs. Of all the fifty states, Hawaii is the very least like any of the others. No wonder it's the first choice as a destination for so many vacationing Americans.

But if Hawaii doesn't look like the rest of America, it's almost a model of what the founding fathers had in mind. It's a place where all kinds of ethnic groups live together and enjoy each other's company. The traditional European stock that settled the first 13 states accounts for slightly more than a quarter of the population of the 50th state, and no one group dominates. Everyone in Hawaii is a member of a minority race!

Even the government is different in Hawaii than in the other 49 states. When it became a state in 1959, Hawaii tossed out its old constitution, which, like every other, had grown cumbersome over the years, and drew up a whole new set of laws. City governments were eliminated completely in favor of county control. Independent school districts were merged together into one state-wide district that insures that all Hawaiian youngsters, no matter how affluent or how poor their neighborhood, get the same quality education. The number of public agencies was cut dramatically, but two new ones were added. An ombudsman, appointed by the legislature but not answerable to it, has wide power that help keep the government honest; and a special auditor keeps an eye on what the bureaucrats are up to in their Honolulu offices.

Until the 1920s most Americans didn't think much about Hawaii. They knew it was out there somewhere, too far away to get excited about. And they knew that it was where you get your pineapples from. Then in 1929, of all years, the Hawaii-based Matson Navigation Company announced the beginning of a weekly steamship service between San Francisco and Honolulu. Depression or no, Americans liked the idea of spending a week at sea, a week in Hawaii and another week on a luxurious cruise ship. But such vacations were more for the idle rich than for the average American.

During World War II, thousands of Americans got there the hard way and went home with a desire to go back. Pan Am had cut the travel time to just a little more than 19 hours from San Francisco even before the war began, but by the time it was over, wartime technology helped them find a better way.

In the late 40s, they were taking as many 45 people at a time from the mainland to the beach at Waikiki in slightly less than 10 hours.

It's quicker these days and bigger planes carry bigger loads. And everyone who makes the trip enthusiastically notes how friendly those Hawaiians are and how pleased they are to have them as part of the family.

Honolulu (facing page), on the island of Oahu, is the capital of Hawaii. Overleaf: (left) the bronze Buddha at the Jodo Mission and (right) Fern Grotto near Wailua.

The Arizona Memorial (previous pages, left) is built over the wreck of the battleship *Arizona*, sunk with 1,102 crew when the Japanese attacked Pearl Harbor. Previous pages: (right) a lava field on the west coast of Hawaii. Above: the beach at Waikiki. Facing page: the west coast of Maui. Overleaf: (left) Ala Moana Park. (Right) the Kalalua Valley.

IDAHO

Gem State

Population (1982): 965,000 (40th)

Size: 83,557 square miles (13th)

Entered Union: July 3, 1890 (43rd)

State Motto: Esto Perpetua (It is Perpetual)

State Flower: Syringa

State Bird: Mountain bluebird

State Tree: White pine

Industry: processed food, wood products, chemical products, metal products

Agriculture: potatoes, sugar beets, wheat vegetables

In California they're proud to point out that they are one of the country's fastest-growing states. Well, Idaho is growing, too, and much of its new population is coming from no less a place than California.

Not many Idahoans are bragging about it, though. One of the things Californians like about them is their conservatism, but they themselves think the invaders from the West are likely to force their liberal ways on them. But in the main, a transplanted Californian in Idaho is more likely to assimilate than proselytize.

Movement from California into Idaho was going on before Idaho was even a Territory. Back in the 1860s when gold was discovered in the northern mountains, a lot of men who had been lured west by the gold strikes of 1849 decided to go back east a bit and have another try.

Southern Idaho was settled originally by Mormons who were convinced they were establishing farms in Utah. They tapped the Snake River to irrigate their farms and in the process turned a desert into one of the country's great agricultural belts.

Irrigation isn't necessary in Northern Idaho, where some people think it rains too much. Like most of the rest of the Pacific Northwest, it does get a bit wet up there, but the result is huge tracts of forest that are not just awe-inspiring, but the basis of a major lumber industry.

In between, the rugged mountains in the middle of Idaho still defy any of man's intrusions. They're beautifully spectacular, but inaccessible to most of us. It's likely that there are spots in the Idaho wilderness no man has ever seen. And passing near to the forestlands on the way to the great ski centers like Sun Valley, it's easy to understand why Idaho was the last of the Continental states to have been seen by Europeans. The Great Event took place in 1805 when the Lewis and Clark expedition crossed the Continental Divide on their way to Oregon.

They were the first white men the Indians there had ever seen, too. Though they liked Lewis and Clark well enough, the Nez Perce Indians who lived on the western slopes of the Rocky Mountains didn't take too kindly to white men in general and were among the most hostile to the idea that they should become Americanized and settle down on a reservation. Naturally, they were finally convinced and by the time the railroads came to Idaho, the fighting was all over. That's not to say nobody at all was fighting. There were bloody disagreements over religion and over cattle-grazing rights; there were labor wars and disagreements over water rights.

It's all over now, of course, and Idaho is a peaceful place. On the other hand, if you're from California and looking at Idaho real estate, it might be a good idea to keep your roots to yourself.

Facing page: Boise, capital of Idaho.

These pages: Boise, with the dome of the Capitol in the middle distance. The
city gained its name from French-Canadian trappers. *Boisé* means "wooded", which
is an apt description of the tree-lined river on which the city was founded.

124

ILLINOIS

The Inland Empire

Population (1982): 11,448,000 (5th)

Size: 56,400 square miles (24th)

Entered Union: December 3, 1818 (21st)

State Motto: State Sovereignty – National Union

State Flower: Violet

State Bird: Cardinal

State Tree: White oak

Industry: electrical equipment, metals, printing, chemicals

Agriculture: corn, soybeans, wheat

There are two things about Illinois that are accepted as an article of faith by anyone who has never seen it: one is that once you leave Chicago, there isn't much else; the other is that what else there is amounts to nothing more than unrelieved prairie.

More than 85 percent of all Illinoisians live in cities, the overwhelming majority in Chicago. But among the population centers that advertising and marketing experts keep an eye on, the so-called Standard Metropolitan Statistical Areas, there are a total of nine in Illinois. Chicago's nearly seven million is a long way from the half million who live in the Illinois portion of the St. Louis-East St. Louis SMSA, but don't forget the importance of that little old lady in Peoria to the folks who need to know what all of America is likely to buy.

On the other hand, 13 of the state's 102 counties are classed as completely rural because they don't have any towns with more than 2500 people.

As for the belief that Illinois is completely made up of prairie land, that's a myth too. It's true that there aren't any mountains, though a hill in the northwest corner rises to 1,241 feet above sea level, and the foothills of the Ozarks in the southern part of the state go a long way toward breaking the monotony. The state got its reputation as a prairie state because it was the first prairie west-bound settlers saw. What they saw when they got a little further west was a bit different. Illinois may have been their first look at the Great Plains, but it was also their last look at tall trees for a while.

If downstate Illinois gets annoyed at all the attention given to Chicago at their expense, they quietly remind you of Springfield and its favorite son, Mr. Lincoln, and then let you turn your eyes northward to that wonderful place on the shore of Lake Michigan. It is the place where modern architecture was developed and the skyscraper invented, and there is no city on earth that seems to understand as well how it should be done. It is the place where people like Sherwood Anderson, Ezra Pound, Carl Sandberg and James T. Farrell shwed the world that America could produce fine writers. It is where American theater flourished and radio and television established themselves as purveyors of entertainment, not to mention that nearly every innovation to come along since the vacuum tube that made it all possible was invented in Chicago.

Chicago is the most American of all American cities. It encourages innovation, applauds greatness, reacts to ideas with unbounded enthusiasm. Which brings up another myth about Illinois: mention the word Chicago in some circles and the word it suggests will probably be "gangsters." The answer to that is that the gangsters have gone. And before he left, Al Capone was heard to say that he never should have left New York in the first place.

Facing page: Chicago's "Magnificent Mile." Overleaf: (left) the Chicago skyline from Burnham Park Yacht Harbor. (Right) the gleaming glass of 333 Wacker Drive.

Above and facing page: the glittering night-time skyline of Chicago, the largest city in Illinois and second largest in the nation. Overleaf: (left) a fountain in front of the Sun-Times Building. (Right) West Lake Street underneath The Loop.

INDIANA

Hoosier State

Population (1982): 5,471,000 (14th)

Size: 36,291 square miles (38th)

Entered Union: December 11, 1816 (19th)

State Motto: Crossroads of America

State Flower: Peony

State Bird: Cardinal

State Tree: Tulip poplar

Industry: metals, machinery, transportation equipment, chemicals

Agriculture: corn, soybeans, wheat

Indiana people agree on a lot of things. They say that corn is the staff of life, that the best thing a person can do on a quiet spring afternoon is to go catch some catfish or sit under a tree and listen to a meadowlark. They don't quite agree that the Indianapolis 500 automobile race should be held on Memorial Day. In fact, they once passed a law against it. They're crazy about high school basketball, they enjoy politics and they love a good storyteller. But don't ask an Indiana native why they call themselves "Hoosiers." There are too many answers to that question.

One is that it comes from a word in the dialect of the nearby Cumberland River area that means "something big." It's true that the Indians the first white men found there were taller than average, but others say that the name comes from a rowdy bunch of hussars that Kentuckians confused with an equally rowdy bunch of Indiana pioneers. Along the same lines, a historian once wrote that Hoosier comes from the disease caused by roundworms that makes men look wild. But today's more civilized Hoosier prefers the explanation that the name is the same as that of a Kentucky developer who went across the border into Indiana to recruit workers. About the only thread that runs through most of the explanations is that the name was given to them by Kentuckians. But in spite of it, they're as proud of the name as they are to be one.

It's the place that produced Booth Tarkington and James Whitcomb Riley; it's where the ultra-conservative John Birch Society was founded and where Will Hayes, the famous censor of so many Hollywood films, cut his political teeth. It's also the home turf of Nelson Algren, Kurt Vonnegut Jr. and Ernie Pyle. Wendell Willkie, the unsuccessful presidential candidate who was one of the first to see America as an International entity, was a Hoosier and so was the great Socialist leader, Eugene V. Debs.

They call the state "the crossroads of America," and a few decades ago, sociologists from Columbia University selected Muncie as the most typically American of all American cities and wrote two bestsellers about life in what they called "Middletown." But if they are thought of as an amalgam of the rest of the country, they are at the same time a breed apart. They're friendly and open and unpretentious; they're citified and disarmingly rural. They're well-educated, too. Purdue University and Indiana University as well as Notre Dame, DePauw and Earlham have seen to that. Probably the best way to describe them is through the words of Irving Liebowitz who said, "Indianans are country smart and their kids are university educated."

Facing page: the Capitol in Indianapolis. Overleaf: (left) the War Memorial and (right) the Scottish Rith Cathedral, Indianapolis.

IOWA

Hawkeye State

Population (1982): 2,905,000 (28th)

Size: 56,290 square miles (25th)

Entered Union: December 28, 1846 (29th)

State Motto: Our Liberties We Prize and Our Rights We Will Maintain

State Flower: Wild rose

State Bird: Goldfinch

State Tree: Oak

Industry: farm machinery, appliances, fertilizers, automobile accessories

Agriculture: corn, soybeans, oats

Some 95 percent of the land is occupied by farms and even many of the people who live in cities and towns are employed in industries that serve farmers. It has almost as many cattle as Texas and more hogs than any other state. It exports more than $2 billion a year in corn, grain and meat. There are other industries in Iowa, ranging from the manufacture of fountain pens to refrigerators, but the land is the thing that seems most important.

It's possibly the only place where Meredith Willson's musical "The Music Man" could have happened. From the very beginning, the population was spread over huge areas, which meant that getting the kids to school was a problem. Most of them went to the famous one-room schoolhouses that are a romantic part of the American past. None of them had to go if it was too much trouble, as it often was, and those who did make the effort didn't learn much beyond the "three Rs" taught to them, usually by a young woman who had herself learned readin', ritin' and 'rithmatic in the same building.

It wasn't until 1902 that the state began to do something to improve things by consolidating schools and providing a means of getting there. But by then, Iowa had also established a state university and an agricultural school. The university had also made history by being the first in the country to admit women.

The first towns in Iowa were established to provide services for farmers and markets for their produce. All of them were on the banks of the Mississippi River and reflected the character of every other river town. All of them, that is, except Dubuque, which had lead mines that attracted a different type of settler. Even today, it is the least typically Iowan of all of Iowa's cities.

Towns in the interior usually became important as country seats. Others were built solely for the convenience of local farmers. In the early days, a farmer needed a place to sell his crops and buy supplies less than five miles from his farmhouse. The result is that Iowa towns, many still not much more than a few houses, a general store and a church, were spaced roughly ten miles apart. When the railroads came, many of them competed vigorously to share the right-of-way and in the process went from small towns to major cities.

Native American inventiveness helped other places grow. Walter Sheaffer put his home town on the map, and on solid financial ground, when he produced his fountain pen in back of his Fort Madison jewelry shop. Fred Maytag did the same for Newton by inventing automatic washing machines.

But in Iowa the land is the thing. It does look good enough to eat!

Facing page: the gold dome of the State Capitol in Des Moines. Overleaf:
(left) Downtown Des Moines from the air and (right) the Capitol.

140

The economy of Iowa is still predominantly agricultural, which makes it easy to believe the state's claim to contain a quarter of the world's grade A topsoil. Some of this farmland can be seen in Crawford County (these pages).

KANSAS

Sunflower State

Population (1982): 2,408,000 (32nd)

Size: 82,264 square miles (14th)

Entered Union: January 29, 1861 (34th)

State Motto: Ad Astra Per Aspera (To the Stars Through Difficulties)

State Flower: Sunflower

State Bird: Meadowlark

State Tree: Cottonwood

Industry: processed food, aircraft, farm machinery

Agriculture: wheat, corn, hay

It's officially known as the "Sunflower State," but most Kansans prefer being associated with the Jayhawk. It's a mythical bird probably made up by Territorial soldiers back in the days before Kansas was a state. It's a fighting bird, with all the qualities of both a jay and a hawk and quite a few all its own. A Kansas historian once said "it is a heroic bird, but don't try to treat it like a hero! You might receive a swoosh from its exhaust." Its most unusual quality is that it flies backwards. The historian explains: "The Jayhawk doesn't care a whoop or two where he is going, but wants to know all about where he has been."

If the Jayhawk is found only in Kansas, the sunflower is not. It became the state flower and its symbol when a Kansas booster visited Colorado and found other visitors from other states all wearing buttons and badges flaunting their origin. He topped them all by picking giant sunflowers and distributing them to fellow Kansans. When he got back to Topeka, he began a campaign to make the sunflower official and won his case in spite of the fact the flower isn't native to his state and was considered by most to be nothing more than a weed or, at best, a source of chicken feed.

But if their bird is a myth and their flower a weed, Kansans have always been proud of their role as innovators. It was one of the first states to let women vote. It pioneered consumer protection laws and public health ordinances. It was first to have its United States senators elected directly by the people and was one of the first to mandate that the name of the candidate should have prominence over the name of the party on election ballots.

About a third of Kansas is almost the same today as it was when west-bound pioneers crossed it a century ago. What's missing are the ten to fifteen million buffalo that ranged over the same prairie. They've been replaced by hundreds of thousands of range cattle brought to Kansas from Texas and Oklahoma, from Montana and Wyoming, to be fattened during the spring and summer on their way to market. It's been a Kansas tradition since the Atchison, Topeka and Santa Fe Railroad made the state the gateway to the marketplace a century ago.

But Kansas isn't all prairie land. It isn't even all flat. It has hills and valleys and sparkling lakes. It has underground caverns and mineral springs. It has one of the greatest concentrations of salt in North America.

What sets Kansas apart, though, is its colorful history. Dodge City keeps some of it alive for tourists, but the people themselves take special pleasure in it. It's why they believe so hard in the Jayhawk. And why one law they all abide by is one passed by an early legislature that ended with the words, "Don't take all this too damned seriously."

Facing page: the State Capitol in Topeka. Overleaf: two panoramic views of Downtown Kansas City.

Above: the Chalk Pyramids at Monument Rocks, south of Oakley. Facing page: some of the rich agricultural land around Wichita. Overleaf: scenes from Dodge City, which still retains its cattle industry, made famous in numerous westerns.

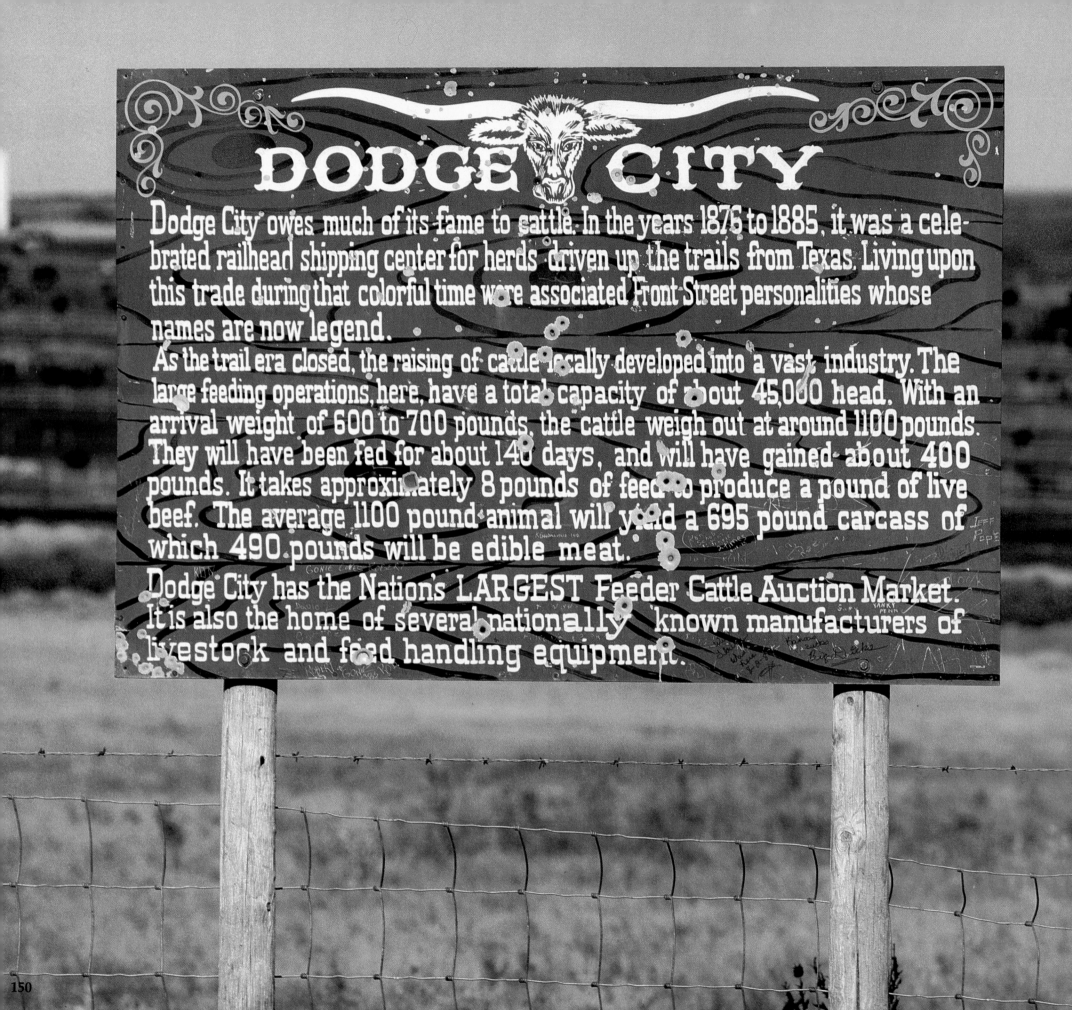

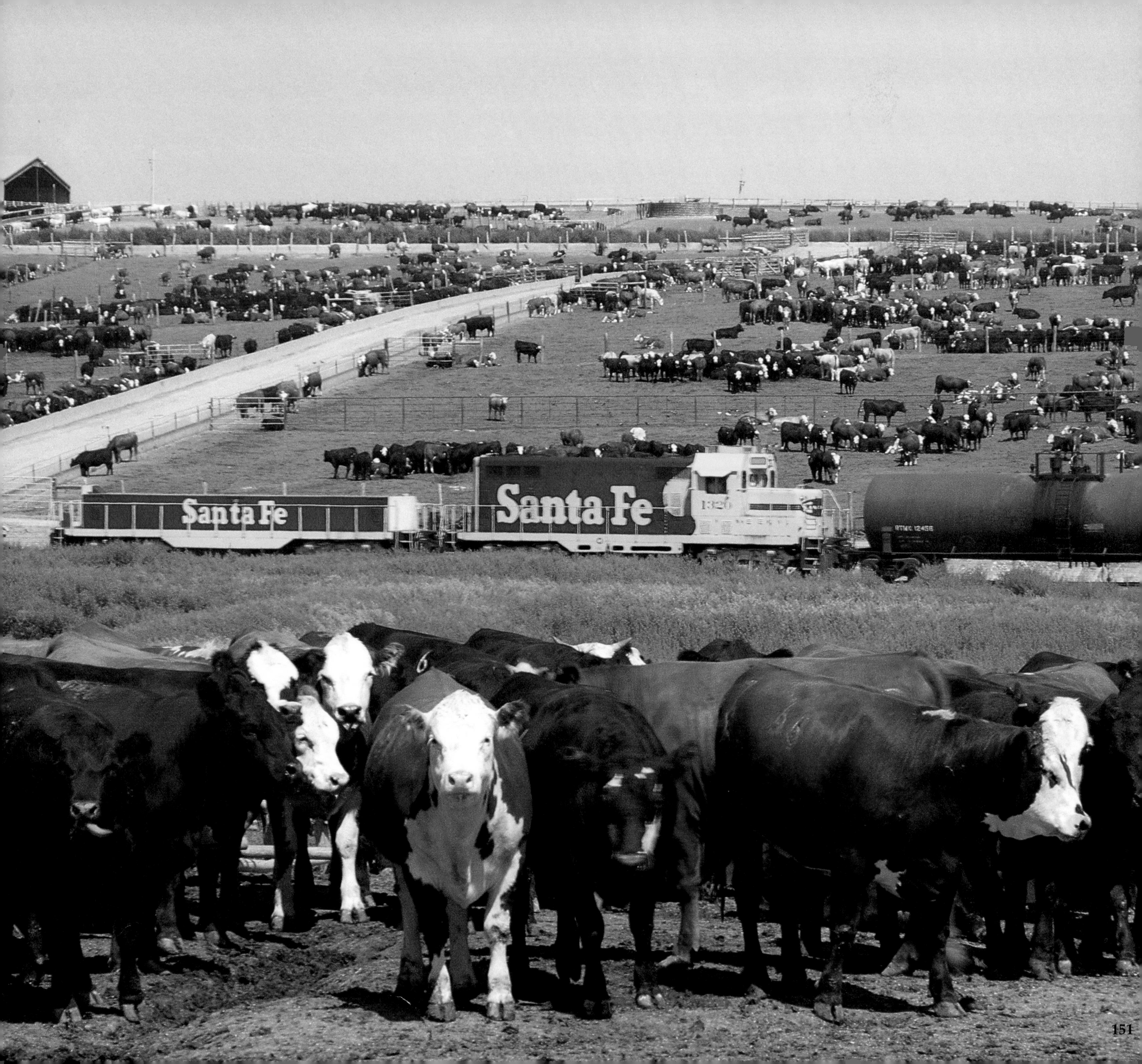
Santa Fe
Santa Fe
1320

KENTUCKY

Bluegrass State

Population (1982): 3,667,000 (23rd)

Size: 40,395 square miles (37th)

Entered Union: June 1, 1792 (15th)

State Motto: United We Stand, Divided We Fall

State Flower: Goldenrod

State Bird: Cardinal

State Tree: Kentucky coffee tree

Industry: distilled spirits, machinery, tobacco, textiles

Agriculture: tobacco, corn, soybeans, wheat

Kentucky is usually regarded as the land of Colonel Sanders and Jack Daniel, of the Kentucky Derby and endless miles of bluegrass. It is also poverty-stricken Appalachia, often provincial and isolated.

Daniel Boone was the first to hack away at the isolation when he began exploring the territory in the mid-18th century. Right through the turn of the century, it was considered the Wild West and thousands moved there anxious to tame it. By the time it was made a state in 1792, it was home to more people than most others. But the same spirit that lured them there in the first place encouraged then to move even further westward as new territories opened up. Among the men who felt the tug was Tom Lincoln, who took his young son Abraham and his wife Nancy west to Indiana and then to Illinois.

Kentucky was neutral in the Civil War, but eventually threw in its lot with the Union. But before that happened, it had sent its sons to fight on both sides. The result was that when the fighting was officially over, blood feuds began in the hills of Kentucky that lasted for generations.

Fighting among themselves in a different way is a point of pride and a long-standing tradition among Kentuckians. Since the day they sent Henry Clay to the United States Senate, they have been crazy about politics and great stump speakers are among the most famous men in the state's history. The politicians play by one rule that makes winning everything. They'll promise you anything, tell you whatever you want to hear. And their constituents love them for it.

On the other hand, once a man has won, then he has a job to do. One former Governor once told an interviewer that there were only two things in life to be avoided: gonorrhea and being Governor of Kentucky. The problem is that as much as Kentuckians enjoy a good political speech, they enjoy the right to go to the public servants for help of all sorts, from getting a road paved to giving their son a little push to get him out of high school. The result is that one shrewd governor generations ago began getting around unreasonable requests by giving away the title of Colonel to what might otherwise have become a disappointed citizen. The title has become more of a real honor over the years, but sometimes just bringing a convention to Louisville is good enough reason.

The image Kentuckians most like to project comes from the thousand square-mile patch of bluegrass in the middle of the state. The great farms like Calumet and Claiborne Stud, Spendthrift and Greentree and the horses they produce are the pride of a nation. Though it's strictly a rich man's game, and there are tobacco farmers in Kentucky who don't know where their next meal is coming from, horse-breeding is a passion shared by nearly everyone in the state. And why not? Nobody does it better.

Facing page: Kentucky State Capitol, in Frankfort.

Previous pages: (left) St. Joseph's Cathedral at Bardstown and
(right) a riverboat on the Ohio River at Louisville. These pages:
some of the rich grazing for which the state is so famous.

LOUISIANA

Pelican State

Population (1982): 4,362,000 (18th)

Size: 48,523 square miles (31st)

Entered Union: April 30, 1812 (18th)

State Motto: Union, Justice and Confidence

State Flower: Magnolia

State Bird: Pelican

State Tree: Cypress

Industry: processed food, chemicals, apparel, electronic equipment

Agriculture: rice, sugarcane, soybeans, cotton

It doesn't even look like the other states. Louisiana is dominated by the Mississippi River, by the Delta, by the city of New Orleans. It has never lost its French flavor and it holds to many of the ideas and customs brought there in the days of Spanish rule. It's the only state that doesn't use the Anglo-Saxon designation of "county" for its subdivisions, but prefers the word "parish," given to it by the Spanish who kept track of people through the churches that served them.

It was a haven for Tories during the American Revolution and slightly later for Acadians driven from Canada, whose descendants still speak their form of French and still live in the Bayous that have sheltered them for more than two centuries.

When the United States bought Louisiana from the French in 1803, it was a territory that extended up the Mississippi River and west to the Rocky Mountains. But New Orleans was considered the real prize and the southern portion of the new Territory was made an independent state less than a decade later.

But statehood didn't change Louisiana much. Their government had been serving them for a century and nobody saw any reason to change, even if it was based on French traditions and the rest of the country had used England as its role model. They went right on speaking French, too, and right into the 20th century Louisiana linguistically resembled present-day Quebec.

By the time the Civil War broke out, the state's population had grown to more than 700,000 and New Orleans was the biggest city in the South. Most of the population were either middle class or working class, but after South Carolina seceded from the Union, Louisiana joined the Southern cause even though a popular election in 1860 proved that the majority was opposed.

Once they did become one of the Confederate States, they sent more than 20,000 of their sons into the fight. The City of New Orleans was captured by the Union Navy in 1862 and the capital was moved to Shreveport, dividing Louisiana and leaving it open for one of the most self-serving governments any state has ever seen. It was a state of affairs that lasted into the 20th century.

It all came to an end in the 1920s in the person of Huey Long, a demagogue of the old school, who was finally assassinated in 1935. Some believe that his methods were worse than the evils he intended to cure, and they may be right. But if he made himself a dictator, he gave the government to the people and gave Louisiana a break with the past that was long overdue.

There is still a lot of the past in Louisiana, more than in most other states, but these days they remember the best parts and at its best this place is nothing short of wonderful.

Facing page: the center of New Orleans and the Superdome. Overleaf: the fantastic floats of New Orleans' Mardi Gras, which are constructed and manned by societies known as "krewes".

It was in New Orleans that the style of music later known as jazz first appeared, and it is in that same city that the music lives on (these pages). The Vieux Carré of the city is noted for its fancy ironwork (overleaf, left), while stern wheelers (overleaf, right) still ply the Mississippi.

162

Above: The Myrtles, a well restored St. Francisville plantation home of 1796. The Old State Capitol (facing page) of 1847 was burned by a Federal army, but was repaired and served as the State House until 1932.

MAINE

Pine Tree State

Population (1982): 1,133,000 (38th)

Size: 33,215 square miles (39th)

Entered Union: March 15, 1820 (23rd)

State Motto: Dirigo (I Direct)

State Flower: White pine cone

State Bird: Chickadee

State Tree: White pine

Industry: paper and wood products, textiles, leather, processed food

Agriculture: potatoes, apples, vegetables

If you were to take a helicopter ride along the Maine coast north from the New Hampshire border to Nova Scotia, you'd travel about 225 miles. If it were possible to walk the coast between the same two points, the distance would be more than 3500 miles. New York and Los Angeles are only 2800 miles apart, and the terrain is an easier hike. There are also more than 200 offshore islands on the Maine coast, adding hundreds more miles to what many regard as the most beautiful seacoast in the world.

But if Maine is linked to the sea, there is more to it that would make it a beautiful place even without the drama of the surf pounding on granite and the spectacular storms the people there call "goose-drownders." It's a place of lush, quiet forests, with meadows carpeted with wildflowers, and sparkling blue lakes. It's dotted with tidy little towns and cities that do all they can to keep their small-town charm.

More than half of the State of Maine is wild and untouched, partly because until very recent times it was inaccessible, but mostly because of the character of the people who call the State of Maine their home.

They prefer to be called "Down-Easters," even though the finger of land they live on is clearly "up" from the rest of the continental United States. It's a term that goes back to the days when Maine was officially part of Massachusetts and the only way to get there was by sailing down the prevailing west wind.

It never was easy to get there, which may help to explain why a real Down-Easter isn't quite like other Americans. They have a reputation for being close-mouthed, for instance, and when they do speak it's in accents not quite like any other. They enjoy a good story, but most sincerely believe in the old axiom: "Laugh before breakfast, weep before supper." But if that implies they are humorless and unfriendly, the picture is not quite accurate. They are probably more like the original New Englanders than anyone living in the New England states today. They believe in thrift and hard work, they are proud of their native horse sense and their ability to survive harsh winters without resorting to the trappings of the 20th century. They believe that cleanliness is next to Godliness, and that Godliness is the most important of mankind's aspirations.

They live closer to nature than most Americans, and they live more by the values we associate with the American pioneers than anybody, including Alaskans.

They have a fierce loyalty to their state, and refer to all other Americans as "Out-of-Staters." It's not that they don't like the rest of us, but they know they have something special that the rest of us will never quite feel no matter how hard we try.

Facing page: Quoddy Head, the easternmost point in the nation. Overleaf: (left) the Androscoggin River at Rumford and (right) Boothbay Harbor. Following pages: (left) Newagen and (right) the Bass Harbor Lighthouse.

MARYLAND

Old Line State

Population (1982): 4,265,000 (19th)

Size: 10,577 square miles (42nd)

Entered Union: April 28, 1788 (7th)

State Motto: Fatti Maschii, Parole Femine (Manly Deeds, Womanly Words)

State Flower: Black-eyed Susan

State Bird: Baltimore oriole

State Tree: White oak

Industry: food products, metals, electronic equipment

Agriculture: tobacco, corn, soybeans

Maryland's northern boundary is the Mason-Dixon Line, which by tradition separated the North and South in the Civil War. But because it surrounds Washington, D.C. on three sides, it was made a military district before it was able to secede from the Union and in the process isolate the Federal Capital.

But is it Northern or Southern? It's still a subject of debate. The real fact is that Maryland is a fascinating combination of both traditions.

It's conservative and solid, at the same time industrious and progressive. It's a place of beautiful mansions on the Eastern Shore that have lured thousands from the North to swap their fast-paced lives for an air of Southern gentility. It's the suburbs of Washington, where middle-class civil servants tend their lawns and raise their kids. It's Baltimore, a city rising dramatically from the years of neglect that created what one of its most famous native sons, H.L. Mencken, called "the ruins of a once-great medieval city." It's a place famous since colonial times for its love of hunting and horse-racing and for the oysters and crabs fresh from the Chesapeake Bay. It's the rugged life in the Cumberland Mountains to the west, the good life in the Potomac Valley.

Its accents are neither Southern nor Northern, and many Marylanders speak with accents that don't even sound American. During the 19th century, nearly as many European immigrants passed through the port of Baltimore as through New York, and many stayed. Though the state was established in 1633 by Leonard Calvert, brother of the second Lord Baltimore, as a haven for Roman Catholics in America, it has always been almost as Protestant as the other original Colonies. Even today, the Catholic population is less than 20 percent of the total.

Though Virginia has for generations kept alive the tradition of being the most English of the fifty states, Maryland is one that strikes British visitors as most like home, and geography is only part of the similarity. Since Colonial days, people in the South and on the Eastern Shore have been devoted to old-world tilting tournaments. The sight of plumed knights in colorful silks jousting for the favor of an equally colorfully-dressed Fair Lady, is still common in many parts of Maryland. The only difference between them and the contests waged by their medieval English ancetors is that all the contestants live to take part in the dancing and revelry that follows every tournament.

New York Times columnist Russell Baker found another similarity when he covered some of the political corruption that for years was a way of life for Marylanders. "The pleasures of the flesh, the table, the bottle and the purse are tolerated," he wrote, "with a civilized understanding of the subtleties of moral questions that would have been perfectly comprehensible to Edwardian Londoners."

Facing page: Baltimore's Inner Harbor, from General Sam Smith Park. Overleaf: (left) the memorial to Mother Seton, the first native-born American to be canonized, at Emmitsburg. (Right) *USF Constellation*, Baltimore.

MASSACHUSETTS

Bay State

Population (1982): 5,781,000 (11th)

Size: 8,257 square miles (45th)

Entered Union: February 6, 1788 (6th)

State Motto: Ense Petit Placidam Sub Libertate Quietem (By The Sword We Seek Peace, But Only Peace Under Liberty)

State Flower: Mayflower

State Bird: Chickadee

State Tree: American elm

Industry: electronics, printing, instruments, machinery

Agriculture: nursery products, apples, corn, tobacco

At least once a year, on Thanksgiving Day, all America is reminded of what we like to call "the Pilgrim Fathers," the people who established the first colony at Plymouth in Massachusetts. In a country without an established aristocracy, generations tried to establish themselves as descendants of the passengers of the Mayflower and, thus, more American than most.

The Pilgrims actually had set sail for Virginia, or at least they said that's where they were going, and claimed to have landed in the wrong place. By having done so, they were free to be independent of the British company that owned Virginia and completely independent of England herself. The rest, as they say, is history.

The history of the United States is preserved in Massachusetts more than anywhere else, especially in the Boston area where the American Revolution began, where the first great stirrings of the Abolitionist movement that led to the Civil War led to lynchings and fiery oratory, where the country's first literary and educational successes let the world know that this was no nation of country bumpkins.

Massachusetts is the state that produced the Adams family and the Kennedy family; it was where the Cabots and the Lowells put an American stamp on the Industrial Revolution. It's the home of Harvard and Amherst and MIT, more universities, in fact than almost any other state. Lexington and Concord, where the War for Independence began, is home today for people who work in one of the world's biggest concentrations of research and electronics facilities.

It's the home of the Boston Symphony and the Boston Pops, of the Berkshire Mountains and hundreds of miles of beautiful beaches. It's quaint little towns and bustling, growing cities. It's Cape Cod and Nantucket and Martha's Vineyard.

For all its rich history, Massachusetts seems right now to be at the peak of its greatness. Though they claimed to be here for religious reasons, the Puritans who established the Massachusetts Bay Colony were hard-headed businessmen and from the very first, their official policies were more oriented toward profit than Puritanism. But religion was important, of course, and when waves of Irish Catholics began arriving after 1845, differences in religion were too important. The old Yankees exploited the newcomers and the newcomers exploited each other.

It is all past history now. Rivalry between ethnic groups has lessened, and though the Massachusetts tradition of individualism is as strong as it ever was, there is more togetherness there now than ever before. And though they like living in small towns and in small houses, the tradition is to think big. And to think young.

Facing page: the State House of Massachusetts, in Boston. Overleaf: (left) the Back Bay area, Boston and (right) an aerial view over Harvard University.

The skyline of Boston takes on a magical air at dusk as the lights
come on and glitter across the Charles River (these pages).

Above: Nauset Beach Lighthouse stands above the sands which gave it its name. Facing page: the colored clay cliffs of Martha's Vineyard. Overleaf: (left) the harbor of Menemsha, on Martha's Vineyard. (Right) Sandwich, the oldest town on Cape Cod.

MICHIGAN

Wolverine State

Population (1982): 9,109,000 (8th)

Size: 58,216 square miles (23rd)

Entered Union: January 26, 1837 (26th)

State Motto: Si Quaeris Peninsulam Amoenam Circumspice (If You Seek a Pleasant Peninsula, Look Around You)

State Flower: Apple blossom

State Bird: Robin

State Tree: White pine

Industry: automobiles, machine tools, chemicals, plastics, metal products

Agriculture: corn, winter wheat, soybeans, fruit, sugar beets

Alaska has the longest coastline of any of the fifty states. That's no surprise. But people are often surprised to find that Michigan is number two. Its coastline runs along the shores of Lakes Michigan, Huron, Superior and Erie. Part of the shore, along the Mackinac Straits, makes Michigan unique in another way, too. it divides the state into two parts, which were inaccessible to each other until 1957 when the Mackinac Bridge connected them.

Michigan is also bigger than it looks on a map of the United States, probably because the lakes themselves are so big. The distance between Detroit in the Southeast corner and Ironwood, up in the Northwest corner, is about the same as the distance from Detroit to New York. Most of Eastern Michigan lies north of Canada's Southern boundary; and Jean Nicolet, the French explorer credited with discovering Michigan, was so certain he had arrived in China that he dressed himself in a Chinese costume before going ashore at Green Bay.

Less than ten percent of all Michiganders live in the Upper Peninsula which, though still beautiful, has been largely robbed of the forests the early explorers saw. The great iron mines and the copper mines, once the country's greatest producers, have been mined out. The extreme South, which in many ways resembles New England, isn't rich in people, either, but those who live there among the lush farms and orchards wouldn't trade it for any other spot.

Though it has a lot of diversified industry, from furniture to paper, the one that affects all the others is Detroit's automotive business. General Motors alone produces about half the passenger cars in the United States, not to mention locomotives, aircraft engines, refrigerators and more. And Detroit is home base to not only GM, but also to Ford, Chrysler and American Motors. Though all of them have plants in others states, a big 35 percent of America's automobiles are produced in Michigan.

But through it all, Detroit is perceived as a dying place, even though it's the fifth-largest of American cities. It has the biggest convention center in the world, part of a new $100 million Civic Center. Its location on the navigable Detroit River with access to the sea through Lake Erie, give it the potential as one of the country's great seaports. But it has problems. The bright side is that Detroit knows it has problems and seems determined to solve them.

And they must be doing something right. Michigan's second largest industry is tourism. To be sure, fewer than Detroit's City Fathers would like to see, as part of their drive to make the Motor City a vacation or convention destination, but more than 15 million people, go there every year for fishing, for skiing or just enjoying the varied landscape. It's a $1.3 billion business and most tourists agree it's money well-spent.

Facing page: Detroit's Jefferson Avenue. Overleaf: (left) the Renaissance Center on Detroit's skyline, and (right) the graceful Ambassador Bridge over the Detroit River.

Water plays a large part in the landscape of Michigan. Above:
Upper Herring Lake near Frankfort and (facing page) the soil-
laden Lower Tahquamenon Falls.

MINNESOTA

North Star State

Population (1982): 4,133,000 (21st)

Size: 84,068 square miles (12th)

Entered Union: May 11, 1858 (32nd)

State Motto: L'Etoile du Nord (The Star of The North)

State Flower: Lady's slipper

State Bird: Common loon

State Tree: Red pine

Industry: food processing, machinery, chemicals, paper

Agriculture: corn, soybeans, sugar beets, wheat

Flying from west to east across the Dakotas and into Minnesota, you don't need to be told when you cross the state line. The landscape turns from brown to green and its fabled lakes reflect the sun into your eyes.

If it looks like a healthy place to live, it probably is. After all, it's the home of General Mills and the Breakfast of Champions, of the Mayo Clinic, where the rich and powerful from all over the world look for cures to whatever ails them, of the Jolly Green Giant and of the great Paul Bunyan, the picture of health if anyone ever was.

Paul Bunyan, the larger-than-life logging man whose big blue ox, Babe, is said to have created Minnesota's lakes by leaving footprints all over the place, is as good a symbol of the Gopher State as anyone. He was a big, friendly guy who could do just about any job that needed doing. So, apparently, were the people who settled Minnesota. They were an interesting combination of Scandinavians and Germans with a heavy sprinkling of New England Yankees. Hard work and clean living, thrift and honesty could easily have become the state motto.

In the state's early days, those qualitites produced many a fortune in timber, iron ore and wheat, but none of those is the key to Minnesota's booming economy today. They've moved forward with the times and prospered in the process. Minnesota Mining and Manufacturing Company is a good example. It went from making sandpaper to Scotch Tape and the whole world wondered how we ever got along without it. Honeywell, another Minnesota innovator, still makes the thermostats that originally built the company, but they're a world leader in the production of computers.

The list of major companies that began in Minnesota and stayed there seems to be endless. Actually, there are 30 such giants, three of which are billion-dollar companies.

Nearly all of them are headquartered in Minneapolis and Saint Paul, the so-called Twin Cities located near the source of the Mississippi River. Though there are some inevitable rivalries between the two cities, they aren't identical twins and either one would be the pride of any other state. Business is good in both, and culture is alive and doing very well in the Minnesota Symphony, the Guthrie Theater, the Saint Paul Chamber Orchestra. Both Minneapolis and Saint Paul cheer for the Twins in baseball, the Vikings in football and the North Stars in hockey, and the only rivalry is associated with the visiting team.

It is the state that gave us Hubert Humphrey and Eugene McCarthy, the Chief Justice of the Supreme Court, Warren Burger, and Associate Justice Harry Blackmun. Minnesotans get involved in national affairs more than most other Americans, but they also stay involved back home. And that, more than almost anything else, is why it's such a terrific place to live.

Facing page: the State Capitol in St. Paul. Overleaf: aerial views of Downtown Minneapolis, with (right) the Hubert H. Humphrey Metrodome.

Through the heart of the Twin Cities of Minneapolis and St. Paul winds the Mississippi (these pages),
passing the university (above) and the First National Bank Building (facing page). Elsewhere in the state
can be found the tumbling waters of the Beaver (overleaf, left) and Gooseberry (overleaf, right) Rivers.

MISSISSIPPI

Magnolia State

Population (1982): 2,551,000 (31st)

Size: 47,716 square miles (32nd)

Entered Union: December 10, 1817 (20th)

State Motto: Virtute et Armis (By Valor and Arms)

State Flower: Magnolia

State Bird: Mockingbird

State Tree: Magnolia

Industry: apparel, transportation equipment, lumber and wood products

Agriculture: soybeans, cotton, rice

Mississippi gave us the writer William Faulkner and the President of the Confederacy, Jefferson Davis. Faulkner found the way of life that was the stuff of his novels, Davis found an attitude that still existed in the 1960s when the state became a Mecca for Civil Rights workers and the inevitable television crews that invaded Mississippi's closed society for the first time in a century.

Conditions are better in Mississippi these days, but it's still the country's poorest state. It has the highest rate of illiteracy and the smallest ratio of doctors. White supremacy as a government policy is only part of the reason. Until 50 years ago, there was a state law forbidding major industry, which represented the evil power of the North, to locate within Mississippi. Cotton was king, and the people who ran Mississippi did all they could to keep it that way.

When cotton farming became a mechanised operation thousands of farm workers found themselves out of work with no prospects, no abilities, no hope. It was bad news for thousands of other people; the ones who ran grocery stores and hardware stores and supplied farmers with other basic necessities of life. By the time the Great Depression hit the United States in 1929, Mississippians could have given their fellow Americans lessons in suffering.

But it all conspired to force the state to reconsider its policies, and small textile factories began dotting the landscape, along with plants that produced such things as furniture and tools. The lure was low wages, of course, and the result was that although people were working, Mississippi stayed at the bottom of the heap in per capita income.

Industries requiring more skill are knocking at the door these days, and the state is responding by funding technical schools.

They're rethinking their agriculture base, too. Cotton isn't king any longer. There are more acres producing soybeans these days. Much of the land is producing cattle and chickens, too; an industry that no Mississippian would have even thought of 50 years ago. But it's an industry that brings $500 million into the state each year today.

Its cities are growing, too, even though the state as a whole has been losing population for decades. There is a good reason: Jackson is a beautiful place that seems to be improving every day. The cities along the Gulf: Biloxi, Pascagoula and Gulfport, are growing faster than almost any other area of the South, thanks to an active tourist industry and a healthy influx of jobs in shipping, refining and the old standby, fishing.

Mississippians don't talk much about the past these days, and the present is only a stop on the way to the future. Most believe the outlook is bright, and they're probably right.

Facing page: heavily buttressed trees standing in the swamp around Desoto Lake, a landscape typical of much of the state.

Above: the push tug *Coral Dawn* displays its work capacity on the Mississippi. Facing page: a modern cotton picking machine, in Coahoma County, which has replaced the hordes of workers. The city of Natchez has some of the finest antebellum architecture in the South, including Glen Auburn (overleaf, left) and Longwood (overleaf, right).

MISSOURI

Show Me State

Population (1982): 4,951,000 (15th)

Size: 69,686 square miles (19th)

Entered Union: August 10, 1821 (24th)

State Motto: Salus Populi Suprema Lex Esto (The Welfare of The People Shall be The Supreme Law)

State Flower: Hawthorn

State Bird: Bluebird

State Tree: Dogwood

Industry: food products, transportation equipment, electronics, chemicals

Agriculture: soybeans, corn, wheat, cotton

In the 1860s, when Missouri was still young, the Secretary of State, William Seward, said: "I see here one state that is capable of assuming the great trust of being the middle man, the mediator, the common center between the Pacific and the Atlantic.

It is right in the middle, and the symbolism of St. Louis as an Eastern city and Kansas City as the spot where the West begins is not something to take lightly. The fact that the two cities are connected by the navigable Missouri River, and that it joins the Mississippi at its half-way point on Missouri's eastern border, makes Seward's remarks seem almost too obvious.

The Ozark Mountains spill over into Missouri from Arkansas, and the people fit the same image as their neighbors to the south; that of being slightly backward backwoods folks who are a little suspicious of other folks who come to see their beautiful hills.

Oddly, they are less "Southern" in their outlook on life than the people who settled the extreme northern part of Missouri, where they still call an amalgam of counties "Little Dixie," though the countryside has more in common with nearby Iowa than any Southern state. On the other hand, there is a little bump of territory in Missouri's southeast corner that looks more like the common vision of Dixie than most parts of Dixie itself.

The people of Missouri came from all sections of the Eastern and Southern United States, but most of them agree that being a Missourian requires a very special quality. They call it "cussedness."

Most of their great-grandparents came from the Deep South on their way north and west in search of independence from the societies established in their home states in the 17th century. Like the immigrants who poured into the Northeast from Europe, they were looking for a new life, but they already had a tradition of independence and wouldn't settle for anything less than allowing the tradition to grow. In the 20th century, we'd call them radicals, or at the very least "nonconformists," but their contemporaries called them "ornery."

It all became intensified during the Civil War, when the state was divided and fought on both sides, often on its own soil. In the end, the orneryness was manifested as suspicion and ever since, no self-respecting Missourian will accept any idea at face value, challenging instead to "show me!"

What they've shown the rest of us is people like Harry Truman and Mark Twain, Casey Stengel and Dale Carnegie. They've shown us better blues singers, the joys of a corn cob pipe and the Spirit of St. Louis. They've shown the way west to thousands, but they also showed thousands that once you're in Missouri, there's no need to go anywhere else.

Facing page: St. Louis' Old Courthouse, framed by the Gateway Arch. Overleaf: (left) the mighty Busch Memorial Stadium, which can be seen again (right) from the top of the Gateway Arch.

Above: the 630-foot-tall, stainless steel Gateway Arch, which commemorates St. Louis' role as the gateway to the West. Facing page: the University of Missouri in Columbia. Overleaf: (left) the Old Courthouse and Gateway Arch, from Downtown St. Louis. (Right) the sternwheeler *Tom Sawyer* on the Mississippi at St. Louis.

MONTANA

Treasure State

Population (1982): 801,000 (44th)

Size: 147,138 square miles (4th)

Entered Union: November 8, 1889 (41st)

State Motto: Oro y Plata (Gold and Silver)

State Flower: Bitteroot

State Bird: Meadowlark

State Tree: Ponderosa pine

Industry: mining, petroleum products, lumber, processed foods

Agriculture: wheat, cattle, sheep

"Montana is everything Colorado thinks it is," says one native. "The mountains are the kind I would create if mountains were ever put on my agenda," said John Steinbeck. "It has a very extraordinary climate," wrote William Clark who, with Meriwether Lewis, led the first expedition into Montana in 1805.

It does have an extraordinary climate. There was a blizzard raging that summer day when Lewis and Clark came on the scene. But they had no idea what it could really be like. In the eastern plains, which cover about two-thirds of the state, the summers are fiercely hot and the winters brutally cold. In the mountains of Western Montana, the ski areas get more snow than the ones further south in the Rockies, and in Northwest Montana the glaciers that give Glacier National Park its name create one of the most beautiful landscapes of any spot in the United States.

They call Montana "Big Sky Country," but they don't seem at all interested in big skylines. There are no big cities there, and the towns most remembered by the more than 4 million tourists who go there each year are the ghost towns that dot the countryside.

If 4 million people a year visit Montana, few of them ever complain about tourist hordes. The operative word in Big Sky is "big." It's possible to spend the entire summer in Montana and see more moose than people. And the people who live there seem to like it that way. Few of their towns are less than 50 miles apart. Its biggest city,

Billings, has less than 67,000 citizens. The capital, Helena, is the smallest of all state capitals, with a population of 24,000.

The result is that Montanans are close to the land and fiercely protective of the environment. They also have a reputation for being hard drinkers, fighters rugged, individualists. But not many states can boast a crime rate as low as Montana's.

On the high plains in the east, there are ranches better described in square miles than in acres, and many are run the old-fashioned way, through hard work on horseback by a father and his sons and a hired hand or two. Many of the spreads are wheat fields that turn a dust gold in the late summer, matching the brown of the dry land out of reach of irrigation.

A surprising number of prairie ranchers and farmers see less of the third of their state that is covered by the mountains that gave it its name than the dudes and ski bums from the East who never know that Montana isn't all beautiful mountains and lakes and lush valleys. Even more surprising is that the people in both ends of the state have roughly the same outlook on life, even though they live hundreds of miles apart in territory that has no family resemblance at all.

For one thing, don't expect to find them at home on a weekend. They're all out enjoying nature. It's something they have in abundance.

Facing page: jagged mountains surround St. Mary Lake in Glacier National Park. Overleaf: (left) marshy grasslands at the foot of the mountains. (Right) the excitment of the bison roundup in Montana.

NEBRASKA

Cornhusker State

Population (1982): 1,586,000 (35th)

Size: 77,227 square miles (15th)

Entered Union: March 1, 1867 (37th)

State Motto: Equality Before The Law

State Flower: Goldenrod

State Bird: Meadowlark

State Tree: Cottonwood

Industry: machinery, chemicals, foods, metal products

Agriculture: corn, soybeans, oats, sugarbeets

Almost all the great westward migrations crossed Nebraska. It was where the Lewis and Clark expedition held its first council with the Indians, where Zebulon Pike convinced the Pawnee that the real Great White Father was an American and not Spanish. It was where the Oregon and Mormon Trails merged and followed the Platte Valley into the West.

It wasn't until 1844 that anybody thought of making it an official part of the United States and they argued about it for ten years before it was all settled. The law that created the Territory of Nebraska along with the Territory of Kansas also led to the creation of the Republican Party at a convention in Omaha in 1858. Their first and most important goal was that there should be "no more slave territory anywhere."

Though they are generally regarded as conservative in their politics, Nebraskans have traditionally voted in ways other Americans are often surprised about. William Jennings Bryan, who began his political career as a Lincoln newspaperman, was the Democratic candidate for president three times.

Whatever they do, Nebraskans are generally united together. Life isn't easy on a prairie farm. It's a continual battle against droughts, grasshoppers, wind and mortgage repayments. It gives them a reputation for rugged individualism, too. The battle unites them as nothing can. Yet in spite of what often seems an uphill fight, more than 85 percent of the population is supported by agriculture, with hogs and cattle accounting for about three-quarters of the income.

The *New York Times* described life there in a special report that said: "They work hard, pay their bills, go to church, spank their children when they think they deserve it, live longer than most Americans and generally believe their way of life is better than any other."

Though the annual cornhusking contest and the state fair and a good rodeo will bring Nebraskans out of any depression, the one thing they love more than anything else is football. But nothing else will do but a game involving the Cornhuskers of the University of Nebraska. The passion began back in the 1920s, when the team was the only one able to beat the great Knute Rockne's Four Horsemen. The Big Red Stadium at Lincoln is one of the biggest of its kind, but that doesn't mean it's easy to get a ticket to one of the games. You'd need to arrange that a year or more in advance.

The phenomenon, according to *Life Magazine*, is "...the bright thread of pride that could lighten even the burdens of drought and depression. Football Sundays are red-and-white sabbaths: Omaha lawyers and ranchers from Chadron recite a shared litany of the team's past glories. Schoolboys and farm wives know every word of 'Dear Old Nebraska U'."

Facing page: the State Capitol in Lincoln. Overleaf: (left) the impressive geological structure of Scotts Bluff, which lies to the northwest of Chimney Rock (right).

Facing page: Omaha's Woodmen Tower and the downtown area from Central Park Mall. Above: Scouts Rest Ranch, North Platte, was once the home of William F. Cody and now forms the focus of the Buffalo Bill State Historical Park.

NEVADA

Sagebrush State

Population (1982): 881,000 (43rd)

Size: 110,540 square miles (7th)

Entered Union: October 31, 1864 (36th)

State Motto: All For Our Country

State Flower: Sagebrush

State Bird: Mountain bluebird

State Tree: Single-leaf pinon

Industry: gaming devices, electronic equipment, mining, chemicals

Agriculture: cattle and sheep, alfalfa, cotton, wheat

Ask anyone who's never explored Nevada what's going on there and gambling in the middle of a vast desert is the most likely answer. For many years before the rest of the country changed its attitude, it was also synonymous with easy divorce. Some might mention Lake Mead and Hoover Dam. A few might think of the ski resorts in the northern mountains.

Yes, ski resorts. Nevada isn't all monotonous dry lakes and desert. There are high mountains in the Northeast and the Sierra Nevada range crosses over from California near Reno and Carson City.

In the last century, there was gold and silver in those hills to lure settlers, and their descendants are still fascinated by the idea that they might strike it rich up there again. Very few native Nevadans don't have tools in the trunks of their cars so they can turn a day's outing into a prospecting adventure.

About 35 percent of all Nevadans earn their living through what they call "the gaming business," and even the smallest of their towns has at least one club where they can go to do a little gaming of their own. In contrast to the glitter of the casinos in Las Vegas and Reno, the local clubs are often typical of the Old West saloons their grandfathers loved so much. Each offers a bar, some offer a general store. All have a couple of slot machines and at least one poker table with a heavy shaded light over it. But that's not to say that Nevadans spend all their time dealing out cards or pulling the handles of slot machines. The local clubs function more as social centers, a place to meet and talk things over.

The big casinos that put Nevada on the tourist map didn't open their doors until after the Great Depression of the early 1930s. By that time, the big gold, silver and copper mines had been played out and the cattle farmers were battling with the sheep farmers over grazing land. The Depression made some of their victories moot.

The early settlers were a lusty lot who enjoyed gambling as much as digging for silver, and the state government decided that was the way to give the economy the boost it needed. When they legalized gambling, they turned Nevada into a tourist Mecca and got exactly the boost they expected.

It all began in Reno with the opening of Harold's Club by an old carnival operator who knew the value of promotion. Highway billboards as far away as New York told the country that there was fun and possible profit waiting for them in the Biggest Little City in The West. Within ten years, Las Vegas, which is easier to reach from Southern California, began developing its world-famous "strip," which includes dozens of elegant hotel-casinos with night clubs and neon lights that have come to symbolize a whole state. But there is more to it than that. Climb up on a lunch counter stool next to a native-born Nevadan and you'll find out.

Facing page: the first sight many people have of Nevada – the Colorado River from the Hoover Dam. Overleaf: day and night views of Fremont Street, Las Vegas.

The city of Reno (above) is smaller than its neighbor, Las Vegas, but is no less concerned with the gambling business. Facing page: Caesar's Palace, Las Vegas, one of the more sumptuous gaming hotels along The Strip (overleaf), officially known as Las Vegas Boulevard.

NEW HAMPSHIRE

Granite State

Population (1982): 951,000 (42nd)

Size: 9,304 square miles (44th)

Entered Union: June 21, 1788 (9th)

State Motto: Live Free or Die

State Flower: Lilac

State Bird: Purple finch

State Tree: Birch

Industry: leather products, wood products, electrical equipment, machinery

Agriculture: apples, dairy products, vegetables

Though regarded by many as typically bucolic New England, New Hampshire has the fourth-largest proportion of factory workers in the country. It is also the fastest-growing state, except for Florida, east of the Mississippi River. Particularly in the south, it is a land of garish shopping malls, high technology industrial plants and condominium developments that are squeezing out some of its quaint New England-style towns.

It is conservative politically, with the result that it is, along with Alaska, unique among the 50 states in not having either a sales tax or an income tax. It is also in the bottom ten in spending for education, for prisons or for welfare.

The philosophy is that the towns, and not the state, and certainly not the Federal Government, should take care of such things. It has been a New Hampshire article of faith since Colonial times. At the begining of the Revolutionary War, it found itself the only New England state still loyal to the Crown and the only one run directly from England. By the end of the War, when there was no more British authority in this part of North America, New Hampshire still hadn't organized its own government. In the confusion, the towns took over and became so powerful in state affairs that, when a legislature was formed, it was organized to include one member for each town regardless of its size. They still operate in New Hampshire that way today and it has the third-largest legislative body in the English speaking world. The other two are the United States Congress and the British House of Commons.

But if its government is peculiar compared to most other states, it was not for nothing that the poet Robert Frost once said "It is restful just to think about New Hampshire." It is a place of fast-moving rivers and deep forests, of majestic granite mountains and restful lakes surrounded by fragrant pines. It is the home state of Daniel Webster, one of the most respected United States Senators in the history of the country, ironically elected by the people of Massachusetts, his adopted state.

Many Americans get an intimate look at New Hampshire every four years when the race for the Presidency begins there in early March. Though the media swears it isn't all that important, that doesn't stop them from braving the cold to troop around the Granite State testing the icy waters to find out who's going to be eliminated from the race in the first Presidential Primary of the year. It all began with the first primaries established right before the First World War. New Hampshire set an early date to beat the spring thaw and its inevitable mud. Over the years, other states have changed their laws to make them first, but the New Hampshire Legislature is always ready to move the date back further if necessary. After all, it's a boost to the economy and outsiders do contribute mightily to the cost of running New Hampshire.

Facing page: a typical covered bridge over the Beebe River at Blair. Overleaf: (left) the smooth granite bed of a stream, and (right) The Pool, both in Franconia Notch.

Lake Winnipesaukee (above) covers some 72 square miles and reflects some of the loveliest scenery in New England. Facing page: the boulder-strewn bed of the Saco River.

238

NEW JERSEY

Garden State

Population (1982): 7,438,000 (9th)

Size: 7,836 square miles (46th)

Entered Union: December 18, 1787 (3rd)

State Motto: Liberty and Prosperity

State Flower: Violet

State Bird: Goldfinch

State Tree: Red oak

Industry: chemicals, electronic equipment, pharmaceuticals, machinery

Agriculture: vegetables, fruit, cranberries, grain

You can drive from east to west in New Jersey in less than two hours and there are plenty of ways to go. You'll find plenty of other people going along. The state highway system handles well over 17,000 vehicles per mile per day. There is one very good reason: though it ranks in the bottom five among all states in terms of size, it ranks number one in population density. There are more than 950 persons per square mile. It's almost as though all those people in cars are looking for a chance to be alone.

But it's clearly not the case. There are beautiful places to go in New Jersey. It's known as the "Garden State," after all.

Its farms are, indeed, more like gardens than the huge spreads in bigger states, but there are a lot of them, stretching from the mountains in the north to the sandy plains in the south. Without them, New Jersey's neighbors in New York City and Philadelphia wouldn't enjoy so many fresh berries, fruits and vegetables. The big cities also rely on rural New Jersey for chickens and milk, even fresh flowers.

The northwestern part of New Jersey is crowned by the Delaware Water Gap, a spectacular gorge cut through the mountains by the Delaware River, which forms the state's western border. The region is largely rural with small towns scattered through the gentle foothills of the Appalachian Mountains.

The eastern border is mainly the Atlantic Ocean with a nearly unbroken string of white, sandy beaches stretching from Newark more than 125 miles south to Cape May. With few exceptions, the towns along the Jersey Shore are Victorian in character as well as in appearance. Many of the communities, like Ocean Grove and Ocean City, and Cape May itself, were founded by fundamentalist Christians who left hard and fast rules for the people who followed them. But rules or no, millions from New York, from Philadelphia and from other parts of New Jersey flock to the Shore and they have a good time doing it. In the last century it was the country's most popular beach, visited by captains of industry, presidents and other important people, all of whom left their mark in the form of stately homes and 19th-century resorts. Today, except possibly for Atlantic City, where gambling is the lure, the "Beautiful People" go elsewhere, leaving the Jersey Shore to a more middle-class aficionado.

The center of the state is charming countryside with huge estates and small college towns. The net effect is almost one of wide-open spaces rather than the high-density the census suggests. More than three-quarters of the land in New Jersey is small towns, woodlands and farms. Of the nearly 7.5 million people who live there, all but about 800,000 live in one quarter of the available space.

(Facing page) a pier at Wildwood, on the Cape May peninsula. (Overleaf, left) the crowded beach at Ocean City. (Overleaf, right) the amusement arcade at Wildwood Crest.

Trenton is proud of its manufacturing businesses, as the bridge (above) declares, and of its gold-topped Capitol (these pages). Overleaf: (left) some of the casinos to be found in Atlantic City. (Right) the interior of the Golden Nugget Casino.

The golden sands of Atlantic City, (above) at Million Dollar Pier and (facing page) near the airport, are among the most popular in the state. Overleaf: scenes around Cape May at dusk.

NEW MEXICO

Land of Enchantment

Population (1982): 1,359,000 (37th)

Size: 121,666 square miles (5th)

Entered Union: January 6, 1912 (47th)

State Motto: Crescit Eundo (It Grows as it Goes)

State Flower: Yucca

State Bird: Roadrunner

State Tree: Pinon

Industry: food, machinery, apparel, lumber, printing

Agriculture: wheat, hay, grain, cotton, corn

The Indians were the first, of course. Then, 400 years ago, the Spanish led by Coronado introduced the first cattle, not to mention Spanish culture; and in the late 1840s, the "Anglos" arrived. Though each blended with the other, they never homogenized, and an Indian rain dance is as common as a Spanish fiesta in this corner of the United States.

Even in this age of sophistication, when Americans know more about each other than ever before, many aren't sure that New Mexico is a part of the United States at all. But it is, and has been since 1912. And people from the other 49 states who haven't seen its seemingly limitless stretches of plain and desert, its rugged mountains, its unbelievably clean air, don't know what they're missing.

One reason for the confusion is that New Mexico didn't grow in the same way as the other Western states. All of the other states were settled in the beginning by migrants from the East and their ties, even though loose, were to the Atlantic Coast. New Mexico's early population, which was well-established even before the Pilgrims set foot on Plymouth Rock, had come from the South. It was run along Spanish feudal lines, with grandees holding huge amounts of territory worked by peons who owed their lives and their livelihood to the "patron."

The development of the Santa Fe Trail brought trappers and traders from the East and the eventual building of the railroads brought even more Anglo-Americans, who put their stamp on the place by changing the names of many Spanish settlements to things more American-sounding.

But today's New Mexico is still a strange, fascinating combination of Old Spain and modern America. In the mixture are 19 Pueblo, 4 Navajo and 2 Apache Indian Reservations. The Pueblo Indians have been there a long time. There is a ruin of one of their settlements at Chaco Canyon that was built in 100 AD.

In 122,000 square miles of territory, only 155 square miles is covered by water, less than any other state. Yet in the high mountains as much as 300 inches of snow fall in a year. But if it's a harsh environment, it is enchanting, even inspiring.

Though it still has one of America's lowest population densities, less than 12 persons per square mile, it is one of the fastest-growing. One reason is tied to an event in the summer of 1945. On July 16, in the desert of Alamagordo, the first atomic bomb vaporized a huge steel tower and the whole world changed forever. Today, New Mexico is the source of about half the uranium mined in the United States, and the industry of atomic research is one of Albuquerque's biggest employers.

Through it all, the caverns at Carlsbad, the Pueblo ruins, the desert, the mountains give New Mexico an atmosphere of a place where time stands still. And what a pleasant atmosphere it is.

Facing page: the adobe church at Taos.

Above: the Mission of San Miguel in Santa Fe, which was begun in 1610 and is, therefore, one of the oldest churches in the country. Facing page: the church of San Felipe de Neri on the Plaza in Old Albuquerque. Overleaf: (left) an example of the cliff dwellings of ancient Indians, which can be found throughout the state. (Right) the subterranean glories of the Carlsbad Caverns.

NEW YORK

Empire State

Population (1982): 17,659,000 (2nd)

Size: 49,576 square miles (30th)

Entered Union: July 26, 1788 (11th)

State Motto: Excelsior (Ever Upward)

State Flower: Rose

State Bird: Bluebird

State Tree: Sugar maple

Industry: publishing and printing, apparel, electrical equipment, photographic equipment, electronics, automotive equipment

Agriculture: apples, beets, cabbage, corn

Most visitors from Europe to the United States spend some of their time in New York City, and many who plan tours before they leave home include a visit to Niagara Falls as a side trip. It's a long day's journey. Though both are in New York State, it's a state about the size of England.

The State of New York resembles England in many places, and that may be one reason why the English were so eager to take it away from the Dutch in the 17th century. But if nostalgia was in their mind, what they really wanted was one of the world's great natural harbors and the territory along the Hudson, one of the world's most important rivers.

The value of both wasn't fully realized until long after it was fully American. In 1825 the opening of the Erie Canal cut the cost of hauling a ton of freight from Buffalo to New York City from $120 to $14. Buffalo, via the Great Lakes, became the gateway to the West, New York City became the gateway to the world. The canal was a boon to much more of the state than just the two great cities at each end. Farmers were able to ship their produce more profitably, and cities across the state became thriving industrial centers.

The great waves of immigration in the late 19th century kept the state prosperous and heavily populated. By the end of the Civil War, New York City had become the financial and banking center of the country as well as the center of the nation's wholesale and retail business.

In the 20th century, it became the country's communications center as well as one of the world's great cultural centers.

But if the statistical evidence shows a state that is completely urban, consider the fact that it ranks in the top ten of all the states in agricultural production. Buffalo produces more flour than Minneapolis, and New York State maple sugar is exported to Vermont, where it is made into syrup and sold as a local product. And given a choice, what restaurant anywhere in the country doesn't proudly advertise its duck specialty as a Long Island native?

And if New York City often seems to be an overwhelming presence, the state has other things to boast about. The first elevator was built in Yonkers, more men's shirts are made around Utica and Troy than anywhere else in the 50 states. The main plant and research center of General Electric is in Schenectady, the headquarters of Kodak is in Rochester and the glass manufactured at Corning is like no other in the world. The Xerox company is headquartered in Rochester, and hundreds of smaller industries, from the manufacture of hats to the production of bricks, keep its title of "Empire State" secure.

But if it is industrial and heavily populated, it's a beautiful place. The train ride from Buffalo to New York, through the Mohawk Valley and down the Hudson Valley is unforgettable. Ask a European tourist.

Facing page: the State Capitol in Albany. Overleaf: the 1,000 Islands Bridge (left) which crosses the St. Lawrence into Canada and (right) the mighty Niagara Falls in winter. Following pages: spectacular aerial views of Manhattan.

NORTH CAROLINA

Tar Heel State

Population (1982): 6,109,000 (10th)

Size: 52,586 square miles (28th)

Entered Union: November 21, 1789 (12th)

State Motto: Esse Quam Videri (To Be Rather Than To Seem)

State Flower: Dogwood

State Bird: Cardinal

State Tree: Pine

Industry: textiles, tobacco products, furniture, machinery

Agriculture: tobacco, peanuts, soybeans, corn, fruit, vegetables

Its Atlantic Coast beaches were the scene of the Wright Brothers' first airplane flight, its rolling Piedmont Hills are the site of all its major cities and most of its population, its Blue Ridge and Great Smoky Mountains are the highest east of the Mississippi River.

The Outer Banks near Cape Hatteras was the first American landfall sighted by Europeans. In 1524, Giovanni de Verrazzano sailed past and noticed a huge body of water just beyond the barrier beach. What he saw was Pamlico Sound, but he couldn't get his ship across the beach and so didn't investigate further. Instead, he drew a map descibing the Sound as the Pacific Ocean and for more than a generation Europeans believed that the two great seas were separated by a narrow strip of sand.

The fact that he couldn't get across the strip became important when settlers finally did come. There is no major outlet to the sea along the Outer Banks and explorers and colonizers bypassed North Carolina in favor of places with better natural harbors.

It wasn't that they didn't try. The first English settlement in the New World was on Roanoke Island, just inside the Outer Banks. Three years after it was established, its inhabitants had vanished without a trace and no trace of them has ever been found. It would be nearly 20 years more before another colony was formed, and it would be north of the first in a more hospitable place they called Jamestown, Virginia.

Colonists began drifting south from Virginia in the 1650s and more, especially Pennsylvanians, followed them. The result was a colony populated by more migrants from other colonies than from the Old Country. Many of their descendants are still there, living in the same parts of the state as their ancestors. Until the 1950s, North Carolina had the lowest percentage of foreign-born citizens and one of the lowest rates of migration in or out.

Industrial development, especially in the textile and furniture business, helped change the pattern and the younger generation, at least, is as likely to be from someplace else as in any state. The change has brought new attitudes, to be sure, but North Carolinians still have a feeling of kinship with each other that makes them unique.

North Carolina was 12th of the original 13 states to join the Union because there was a strong feeling against a big central government. Yet it was one of the last of the Southern-oriented states to secede from the Union.

Loyalty is the underlying reason for both. North Carolinians are proud of their state. You can hear it in their official state song:

"Though the scorner may sneer at, and witlings defame her,
Yet our hearts swell with gladness whenever we name her."

The buildings of Winston-Salem (facing page) reveal their European heritage, as do those of Old Salem: (overleaf, left) a shoemaker's shop and (overleaf, right) Elm House Tavern, which first opened its doors to travelers in 1784.

The Great Smoky Mountains National Park (these pages) covers some
half a million acres of densely forested hills and mountains
along the Tennessee border.

NORTH DAKOTA

Sioux State

Population (1982): 670,000 (46th)

Size: 70,665 square miles (17th)

Entered Union: November 12, 1889 (39th)

State Motto: Liberty and Union, Now and Forever, One and Inseparable

State Flower: Prairie rose

State Bird: Meadowlark

State Tree: American elm

Industry: processed food, farm machinery

Agriculture: wheat, soybeans, oats, potatoes, sugarbeets

Though trappers and traders had been criss-crossing the territory for decades, and a few small settlements had been established along the Valley of the Red River of the North by farmers and adventurers heading west from Minnesota, North Dakota didn't loom large as a place to settle down and take root until 1871, when the Northern Pacific Railroad began a promotion campaign to sell the land across its newly-opened right-of-way.

The Railroad opened an office in London as a base for agents who fanned out all over Europe distributing brochures about opportunities in North Dakota. They had a similar office in New York, and set up huge reception centers for the anticipated wave of immigrants.

Though they offered a good deal, a spread of land at $2.50 an acre for a 10 percent downpayment with seven years to pay the balance and a free train ride to their new home, they sold just 46,000 acres in 14 months, and all the land they sold was in Minnesota.

New ways of milling flour put Minnesota on the map a few years later and the demand for more and more wheat changed the whole picture. Between 1878 and 1890, North Dakota not only became a major producer of spring wheat, but its population grew 1000 percent.

The winters are cold in North Dakota and the summers are hot. Most of its settlers had come a long distance, in many cases from Norway, from Germany, from Russia. They were mainly poor and eager to change their lives. The great open spaces, the harsh extremes of the weather, separated the weak from the strong and created a new breed: The North Dakotan.

Loneliness and isolation make friendliness and courage vital. The simple act of surviving makes optimism one of their traits. And because wheat farming is a seasonal occupation, most of the new North Dakotans had time for reading and both the time and the need for the human contact of social organizations.

The result is that today's attitude among the people of North Dakota isn't much different than it was in 1902, when a Fargo clergyman wrote of them: "Though they are new here, they consider themselves North Dakotans. They feel it, they boast of it! Soil and climate and circumstances are doing their work. The boundless stretch of prairie from sunrise to sunset, the cloudless skies, the long winter nights and the long summer days, the ever-singing wind, the prodigal wealth of wheat and flax... all these mold and color humanity. So in the North Dakotan one finds a man prompt, generous, speculative, ready to learn each new thing, hard to tie to anything, but, when tied, staunch, sturdy and loyal."

Facing page: an aerial view of Bismarck, North Dakota's state capital. Overleaf: (left) some of the rich agricultural land around Williston. (Right) the International Peace Garden at Dunseith.

OHIO

Buckeye State

Population (1982): 10,791,000 (6th)

Size: 41,222 square miles (35th)

Entered Union: March 1, 1803 (17th)

State Motto: With God, All Things Are Possible

State Flower: Scarlet carnation

State Bird: Cardinal

State Tree: Buckeye

Industry: machinery, metal products, transportation equipment

Agriculture: corn, hay, wheat, soybeans

One of the things that bothers an Ohioan more than almost anything is that most other Americans consider them part of the Midwest when they are clearly, they say, an Eastern state.

The truth of the matter is that Ohio isn't Eastern or Western, Northern or Southern any more than it is Midwestern. It's an interesting combination of all of them, which makes it typically American.

The mountains of Pennsylvania and West Virginia sweep into Ohio from the east and become gentle hills and beautiful valleys and then broad plains that roll into Indiana on the west. The broad Ohio River gives it its southern boundary and more than three-quarters of its northern border is the shore of Lake Erie.

The Indians who were there first didn't give it up easily. The French and the English fought over its strategic location as the key to the West, and when the West was won, Ohioans found out for themselves how important those battles were.

Though Ohio farmland was the richest many early settlers had ever seen, the late 18th century, when they began arriving in huge numbers, was also the beginnings of the Industrial Revolution. The rivers that had made it so easy to get there in the first place also made it easy for Ohio to get in on the ground floor in the race towards industrialization. By the beginning of the 19th century, Cincinnati was the first industrial city in the American West. It was making saddles and guns and windowglass, milling flour and making salt. By 1840, the state's manufacturing output accounted for a quarter of its economy and it was third biggest of all manufacturing states. It's been that way ever since and Ohio produces everything from rubber and steel to breakfast food and soap. It's the home of Procter and Gamble, the birthplace of John D. Rockefeller, Sr., of Thomas Edison, B.F. Goodrich and Charles Kettering, not to mention the Wright Brothers.

Ohio is the third largest industrial state, yet it ranks 11th in agriculture. It has more than a half-dozen cities any state would consider "major," and well over 100 more that no one would ever accuse of being small towns. But most Americans think of Ohio as Small Town America, just as they think of it as Midwest America.

Ohio grew in a hurry, with people pouring in from every direction at once and settling down. It didn't have time to establish traditions and folkways, there was growing to do. The result is that, in spite of what other Americans might think, there probably is no such thing as a typical Ohioan. But if they have problems of identity, they have a common goal. It was established for them in the 1830s when one of their leaders wrote: "Our position in the Nation is peculiarly felicitous as to soil, climate and productions, and it will be our own fault if we are not the happiest people in the Union."

Facing page: government offices on the east bank of the Scioto River in Columbus. Overleaf: (left) Downtown Cleveland, and (right) a marina at Vermilion, on Lake Erie.

Cincinnati (these pages) had humble origins as the tiny
settlement of Columbia in 1788, but it is now a thriving
industrial town with well over a million inhabitants.

OKLAHOMA

Sooner State

Population (1982): 3,177,000 (25th)

Size: 69,919 square miles (18th)

Entered Union: November 16, 1907 (46th)

State Motto: Labor Omnia Vincit (Work Conquers All Things)

State Flower: Mistletoe

State Bird: Scissortailed flycatcher

State Tree: Redbud

Industry: oil field equipment, food products, minerals

Agriculture: wheat, cotton, sorghum, peanuts, pecans

In the mid-19th century when white men were filling up the territories that would become the American Midwest, a lot of Indians were moved off their land and a place to put them became a national problem. It wasn't a problem too many people lost any sleep over, though. There was a strip of territory north of Texas and south of Kansas that was criss-crossed with cattle trails and waggon roads. It was home to five tribes of Indians who had become "civilized" enough to live under their own laws, which were similar enough to the white man's laws that many thought the Territory would eventually become an Indian state within the Union. Possibly with that in mind, the Federal Government bought some of the Indian land and began moving some of the surplus red men into the area.

In the process, surveyors discovered a hole in the middle of the map that had never been explored. It gave a group of Kansas wheat farmers an idea. They would not only explore it, but they'd settle it. By the 1870s mechanization had made it necessary to have huge spreads of land to make a profit on wheat, and there was plenty of it in the Indian Territory, even if it hadn't shown up on the map.

Those first white men called themselves "boomers," and the boom they created was heard all the way back in Washington. It wasn't long before the Government began buying more surplus land from the Indians, this time for white farmers and ranchers. The idea of a separate Indian state was clearly one whose time had passed.

The land the Government bought was declared open for homesteading. It would be sold, for the same $1.25 an acre paid to the Indians, to any American citizen, male or unmarried female, over the age of 21, or any alien intending to become a citizen. Anyone who already owned more than 160 acres didn't qualify, and no one could get a valid title to the property without first living there for five years. Everybody was entitled to a "quarter section," a quarter of a square mile, and sections were allotted on a first-come, first-served basis. The result was a mad rush that was repeated several times, each time bringing thousands into the Territory that would in 1907, when statehood came to Oklahoma, give it a population of nearly 1.5 million.

The state still has a frontier spirit that judges people on what they've done lately rather than where they came from and what they brought with them. Will Rogers, a son of the Cherokee and an Oklahoman, is often a role model for the people who call themselves "sooners," after the folks who moved in slightly ahead of the homesteaders to get the best homesites. One of the dozens of memorials to him has an inscription that sums up not only his, but his fellow Oklahomans' formula for surviving: "He was born with a gift of laughter and a sense that the world was mad."

Facing page: the State Capitol Complex in Oklahoma City. Overleaf: (left) a cattle auction in Oklahoma City and (right) farming land north of the city.

Above: Downtown Oklahoma City. Facing page: some of the
futuristic architecture for which Tulsa's Oral Roberts University
is so justly famous.

OREGON

Beaver State

Population (1982): 2,649,000 (30th)

Size: 96,981 square miles (10th)

Entered Union: Februaury 14, 1859 (33rd)

State Motto: The Union

State Flower: Oregon grape

State Bird: Meadowlark

State Tree: Douglas fir

Industry: lumber and wood products, food products, machinery, printing

Agriculture: wheat, hay, potatoes, fruit

It rains a lot in Western Oregon. On the other hand, it doesn't rain enough in the eastern part of the state. The reason is a beautiful one: the Cascade Mountains. They cut Oregon into two unequal parts, with lush countryside in the west, high desert in the east and they give the state some of the country's most wonderful mountain scenery.

Between the Cascades and the Coastal Range, the Willamette Valley is home to the large majority of Oregonians who are younger, on average, than people in most other states and more fiercely-protective of their environment than almost any other. They have good reason. Oregon has everything. West of the Coastal mountains, a strip as much as 25 miles wide along the Pacific Ocean is rich farms and forests that often end on white sandy beaches or on rocky cliffs that are perfect for watching the sea-lions who love the Oregon coast as much as anyone.

As much as the landscape itself is varied, there may not be such a thing as a typical Oregonian. The first settlers were fur traders and lumbermen and missionaries, some of whom were living on the Oregon coast at the begining of the 19th century, when the American Western Frontier was way back in Indiana.

The Lewis and Clark Expedition, which reached the headwaters of the Columbia River in 1805, opened the Oregon Trail which took thousands west after the Civil War. The trail had two branches, one leading into California, where there was gold, the other into Oregon, where there was rich farmland. The branch a pioneer took depended on his vision of the future.

The ones who took the northern route were generally craftsmen and farmers, and others who would put a conservative stamp on the population. The WPA guide to Oregon, published in 1940, said of them: "They came because they thought they might better themselves and their families. No sane person would ever question their courage, or the hardihood of those who survived; but it is barely possible that they were not all either sunbonneted madonnas, or paragons of manhood jouncing westward with banjoes on their knees."

But, of course, they weren't the last of the immigrants, and although many parts of Oregon look like New England, thanks to the architectural taste of the early settlers, the similarity is only skin deep. As the WPA guide points out, "the individual Oregonian may be certain that he understands himself, but he cannot always be so sure of his neighbors."

And since those words were written, Oregon has changed even more. By 1970, it was growing so fast the governor told a group of visitors: "Travel, visit, drink in the great beauty of our state. But for God's sake, don't move here!" It was an attitude that changed again in the 1980s. But one attitude remains. If you move there, be prepared to love it and protect it. That's become an Oregon tradition.

Facing page: the distinctive State Capitol in Salem. Overleaf: (left) Sunrise Lodge, a popular skiing venue on the slopes of Mount Bachelor. (Right) Portland, the "City of Roses" is the state's largest city.

Above: the Columbia River Gorge cuts its way through the mountains. Facing page: the Yaquina Bay Bridge at Newport. Overleaf: (left) the snowclad summits of Three Sisters and Broken Top. (Right) Wizard Island, a symmetrical volcanic cone, rises 760 feet clear of Crater Lake.

PENNSYLVANIA

Keystone State

Population (1982): 11,865,000 (4th)

Size: 45,333 square miles (33rd)

Entered Union: December 12, 1787 (2nd)

State Motto: Virtue, Liberty and Independence

State Flower: Mountain laurel

State Bird: Ruffed grouse

State Tree: Hemlock

Industry: steel, food processing, apparel, machinery

Agriculture: mushrooms, corn, hay, apples, tobacco, vegetables

In 1984, a special act of Congress made William Penn an American citizen. He would have been proud. In 1681, after having been granted a tract of land in North America that the king called Pennsylvania, he wrote: "Tis a clear and a just thing, and my God that has given it to me through many difficulties, will, I believe, bless and make it the seed of a nation."

Pennsylvania was the result of a dream in Penn's life to establish a true melting pot, a "holy experiment" that would bring together people of all races and persuasions. He said that "man is a better creature when he is free, and freedom flourishes best in a diversified society."

One hundred years later, when the new nation was established at conventions at Philadelphia, Penn's experiment had been proven successful, and his ideas became the backbone of what the new country would stand for. In fact, the experiment had worked so well, the other 12 colonies looked to Pennsylvania to help them resolve the differences among them, earning it the nickname, the Keystone State.

Through the 19th century and well into the 20th, Pennsylvania was one of the world's great industrial powers, producing such millionaires as Andrew Carnegie and J.P. Morgan, Andrew Mellon and Charles Schwab. It also provided the battleground for the emergence of organized labor in the years between the two world wars.

But though nearly 70 percent of all Pennsylvanians live in urban areas, the state still has almost 17 million acres of forest land, a reminder that it is still "Penn's Woods," and the farm country in the Southeast is not only among the richest on the Eastern Seaboard, but a genuine tourist attraction as well. They call it "Pennsylvania Dutch Country." It's a remnant of Penn's Holy Experiment.

William Penn cast his net all over Europe looking for colonists, but he found the most fertile ground among the German and Swiss Protestants who were united culturally but divided into religious groups known by such names as Mennonites and Dunkers, Moravians and Schwenkfelders. In Pennsylvania, everyone called them Pennsylvania Dutch, from the word *Deutsch*, meaning German.

Over the years, they have remained true to the traditions of their ancestors, keeping the old customs and folklore and working those incredibly rich farms by the same methods used in the 18th century. They themselves are one reason for visiting Pennsylvania, but once the curiosity has been satisfied, tourists come back again and again. The beautiful, peaceful countryside becomes more of a lure. On the other hand, the people sum up what makes Pennsylvania what it is. From the very beginning, Pennsylvanians have been free to remain individualistic in the melting pot, and there are few places in America where such an idea works so well. It all goes back to William Penn, who said: "We must *give* the liberties we *ask*."

Facing page: statues and cannon litter the battlefield of Gettysburg, the conflict generally recognized as the turning point of the Civil War. Overleaf: Philadelphia: (left) Benjamin Franklin Parkway and (right) Independence Hall, where the Constitution was written.

Facing page: Philadelphia's City Hall. Above: central Pittsburgh as seen from Mount Washington. (Overleaf) the traditional farming techniques which still survive in Amish country, around Lancaster.

305

Facing page: Pennsylvania's Grand Canyon, the 50-mile-long and 1400-foot-deep gorge of Pine Creek. Above: Main Street in Jim Thorpe, a town in the eastern part of the state. Overleaf: (left) the Pennsylvania Memorial at Gettysburg.

RHODE ISLAND

Ocean State

Population (1982): 958,000 (41st)

Size: 1,214 square miles (50th)

Entered Union: May 29, 1790 (13th)

State Motto: Hope

State Flower: Violet

State Bird: Rhode Island red

State Tree: Red maple

Industry: jewelry, machinery, textiles, electronics

Agriculture: potatoes, apples, corn

There are so many farms and forests, wetlands and bays in Rhode Island, it's hard to believe that it is the smallest of the 50 states. Though it is only 48 miles from the northern to the southern tip, it has 76 miles of Atlantic Ocean shoreline and 170 miles of coastline on its inland waters. Narragansett Bay, extending from Newport to Providence, is bordered by hills and pastureland and dotted with small, peaceful towns. The overall effect is that there is plenty of room to spread out in Rhode Island.

It all began in 1636, when a clergyman named Roger Williams had a falling out with the Massachusetts Puritans and moved down to the head of Narragansett Bay to found a more liberal colony at Providence. Within ten years, others had followed him and there were thriving towns at Newport, Warwick and Portsmouth, too. They eventually banded together and Williams secured a Royal charter to make it all legal. The city of Newport had been settled by John Clarke and William Coddington, who had been banished from Massachusetts for their liberal tendencies regarding religion. They bought an island in the Bay that the Indians who sold it to them had called Aquidneck. Before long they changed its name to the "Isle of Rhodes," which later became the basis for the name of the whole state. The suggestion had come as far back as 1524, when the explorer Verrazano landed on Block Island and noted in his log that it reminded him of the Mediterranean island of Rhodes.

The lure of true religious freedom brought hundreds to the new colony and Rhode Island quickly shifted from farming to ship building and seafaring. In the years before the Revolutionary War, Newport was the center of the slave trade and in the process became one of the wealthiest cities in America. In spite of it, the state outlawed slaves in 1774, almost 35 years before the rest of the country followed suit.

Privateers took up the slack and made Newport wealthier still, and by the 1760s it was the resort of choice for plantation owners from the South and from the West Indies who went north to escape the heat of the summer. Even though the city went into decline as a major port after the Revolution, the tourist wave continued and after the Civil War, Ward McAllister, a former Southerner who had known Newport as a youngster, set himself up as the organizer of New York society and lured the likes of the Astors and Belmonts to the city at the end of Narragansett Bay.

The houses they built to demonstrate their wealth are what lure tourists there today, but the real lure is what it has always been, a unique combination of wild seascapes and peaceful landscapes.

Built on an island, Newport has great communication problems, which have been eased by the Newport Bridge (facing page and overleaf, left) across Narragansett Bay. Overleaf, right: yacht harbor at Newport.

SOUTH CAROLINA

Palmetto State

Population (1982): 3,203,000 (24th)

Size: 31,055 square miles (40th)

Entered Union: May 23, 1788 (8th)

State Motto: Dum Spiro Spero (While I Breathe, I Hope)

State Flower: Carolina jessamine

State Bird: Carolina wren

State Tree: Palmetto

Industry: textiles, chemical products, machinery, apparel

Agriculture: tobacco, corn, soybeans, cotton, fruit

There are really two South Carolinas. In the beginning, settlements began in what the natives call "low country," a coastal plain that is protected from the sea by a chain of barrier beaches they call "sea islands." The plain gives way eventually to the hills of the Piedmont, which South Carolinians call "up country." The people who live there are as different from their neighbors on the coast as both are different from North Carolinians.

The sea islands, including Hilton Head, one of the Southeast's great resorts, stretch from Savannah to Myrtle Beach. They alternate between tidal swamps and higher savannahs, whose rich black soil produced spectacular cotton crops for antebellum plantation owners. As the plain marches inland, rice and indigo plantations dot the landscape. In the hills beyond, where America's first cowboys once herded cattle, modern America rears its head in the form of industrial plants, shopping centers and tract housing.

But from the very beginning, the symbol of South Carolina, and in many ways of the entire South, is the City of Charleston. In Colonial times it was the country's most important port south of Philadelphia, but it was a city like no other. As an important port it produced families of great wealth, but unlike other American cities, the wealthy became the aristocracy. reflecting the social patterns of London. They lived the good life, sent their children to Europe to be educated, advanced culture and spread their influence inland.

In 1860, when appeals for secession from the Union were being heard all over the South, the up country farmers didn't agree and Charlestonians were beginning to doubt their influence. But they all came together on April 12, 1861 when the batteries at Charleston opened fire on the Federal Fort Sumter across the harbor.

The act may have united South Carolina, but it started the War Between the States and ended South Carolina's Golden Age. Fortunately, the City of Charleston itself survived the war untouched and today it is a city full of treasures, with some 75 pre-Revolutionary War buildings included in a total of some 850 that were there the day the cannons opened fire to change the course of history.

If they respect the past in South Carolina, they have a healthy regard for the future. It was the first of the Southern states to accept, even become enthusiastic about, racial equality in the 1960s, and in the years since it has become a model for other states, even some Northern states, to follow.

Back in 1650, Sir Walter Raleigh said that South Carolina was "God's earthly paradise," with perpetual spring and summer; "a garden shaded by palm trees." He was wrong about the palm trees, but anybody in South Carolina will forgive him that one mistake.

Facing page: Charleston's St. Michael's Episcopal Church, in which the first service was held in 1761. Overleaf: two graceful old buildings in Charleston: (left) the Dock Street Theater and (right) the Joseph Manigault House.

Above: Drayton Hall, one of the state's many graceful antebellum plantation houses. Facing page: Charleston.

SOUTH DAKOTA

Coyote State

Population (1982): 691,000 (45th)

Size: 77,047 square miles (40th)

State Motto: Under God, The People Rule

State Flower: Pasque flower

State Bird: Ringnecked pheasant

State Tree: Black Hills spruce

Industry: apparel, metals, machinery, glass and pottery

Agriculture: wheat, corn, soybeans, hay, flax, barley

They look alike on the map, and they sit one on top of the other. But don't ever make the mistake of lumping North and South Dakota together as "The Dakotas." Especially in South Dakota where they feel more kinship with their neighbors in Nebraska and, in fact, never, ever, relate to the wheat farmers to the north. Except that the farms in South Dakota are more likely to produce corn and support cattle and there are twice as many sheep there as people, it's only natural that most Americans consider North and South Dakota the same. They look alike.

In the east, where the populations are centered, the farms run along rich river valleys. In the west and center, the land is more hostile and drier.

South Dakota has more Indians, too. More than any other state on the Great Plains, in fact. This is where the great war between the U.S. Cavalry and the Sioux came to an end with the death of Sitting Bull and the dreadful massacre of hundreds of Indian men, women and children at Wounded Knee in 1890. In the nearly 100 years that have passed since, the wounds haven't healed and still divide red from white and many of the Sioux from each other.

One of the great Sioux leaders, a native of South Dakota's Black Hills named Crazy Horse, is the subject of a monumental unfinished sculpture planned to have been 563 feet high, carved out of the side of a mountain. It was the work of sculptor Korczak Ziolkowski, who accepted a 1936 challenge by an Indian chief to "caress a mountain so that the white man will know that the red man had great heroes too."

The challenge grew out of another South Dakota monument that lures some 2 million visitors a year to the state. It is Mount Rushmore, where another sculptor, Gutzon Borglum, carved 60-foot-high representations of Presidents Washington, Jefferson, and Theodore Roosevelt on the side of another mountain.

Most of those 2 million tourists also pass through the hills early pioneers called Badlands and General Custer called "Hell with the fires burned out." And few miss the town of Deadwood, which has more past than present, but whose past includes the funerals of Calamity Jane and Wild Bill Hickok.

The Lewis and Clark Expedition spent the winter of 1804-5 in South Dakota, and though they found their great Indian guide Sacajawea there, they wrote off their surroundings as part of "The Great American Desert." Though they were keen observers, and right about most things, they were wrong about South Dakota. More than 41,000 farms support about three-quarters of the people who live there, and anyone who lived through the disastrous 1972 flood near Rapid City would have to smile at that part of the Lewis and Clark Journals. But with typical South Dakotan patience, a local historian explained: "The Expedition chanced to occur during an extended period of severe drought."

Facing page: the State Capitol in Pierre, completed in 1910. Overleaf: (left) Mount Rushmore, where the heads of four Presidents have been carved out of the solid mountain. (Right) River Valley Cedar Pass, in Badlands National Park.

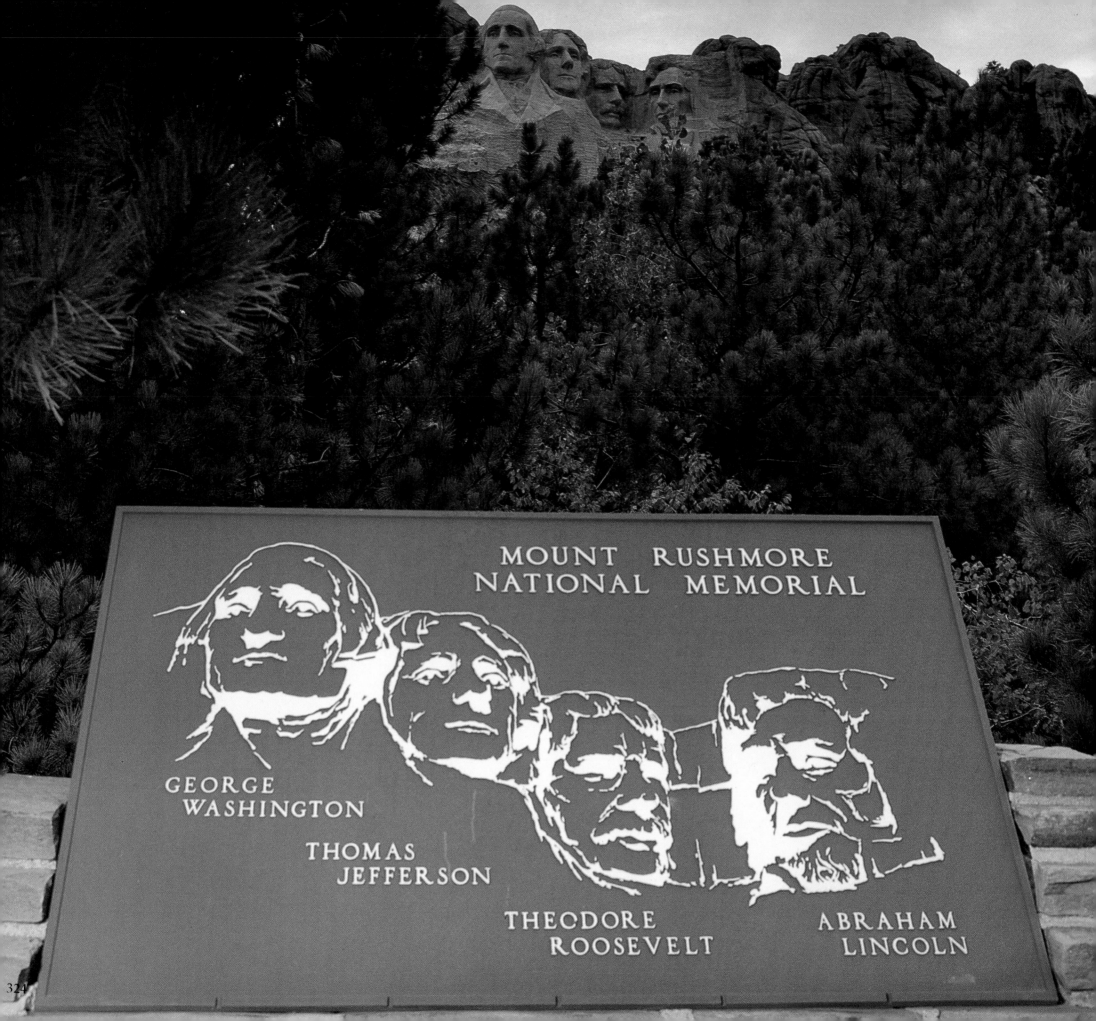

MOUNT RUSHMORE
NATIONAL MEMORIAL

GEORGE
WASHINGTON

THOMAS
JEFFERSON

THEODORE
ROOSEVELT

ABRAHAM
LINCOLN

Lake Oahe was formed by damming the Missouri at Pierre and is
crossed by United States Highway 12 (above) near Mobridge.
Facing page: wagon compound in Custer State Park.

TENNESSEE

Volunteer State

Population (1982): 4,651,000 (17th)

Size: 42,244 square miles (34th)

Entered Union: June 1, 1796 (16th)

State Motto: Agriculture and Commerce

State Flower: Iris

State Bird: Mockingbird

State Tree: Tulip poplar

Industry: apparel, chemicals, machinery, food products, electronics

Agriculture: soybeans, tobacco, cotton, wheat

It's the birthplace of Elvis Presley and the Grand Ole Opry, of Davy Crockett and Sam Houston. It extends from the heights of the Smoky Mountains to the bottomlands of the Mississippi River. It's a place where some people live very much like their predecessors who fought the Cherokee and Chickasaw Indians for their farms, and where nuclear physicists have found a nice place to live.

Much of Tennessee didn't come into the 20th century until the century was three decades old and the Federal Government began building hydroelectric projects in the Valley of the Tennessee River. Though seven states share the benefits of the Tennessee Valley Authority, Tennessee is the major beneficiary of the program that provides low-cost electricity for rural areas and industrial centers as well as flood control, land conservation and river navigation.

TVA united the states it serves, but it also united Tennessee itself. In a way. Because the state is divided from north to south by mountains and valleys into three distinct regions, the only groups that were ever united before were the Middle and West, and that was a fragile union at best. The people in the West, who sided with the South in the War Between the States, are as different from East Tennesseans, who fought with the North in the War, as an Appalachian farmer is from a Mississippi planter. Some people in the eastern mountains still regard West Tennessee as a worthless swamp; some in the Middle section, where they raise fine horses and rich tobacco, think both East and West lean too far North. It's hard to forget the Civil War in Tennessee. There are reminders everywhere in places with names like Chickamaugua, Shiloh, Chattanooga and Nashville. More than 600 major battles were fought in Tennessee, some of the bloodiest of the War.

In the years before the War, Tenessee was thought of as the wild frontier, personified by one of its sons, President Andrew Jackson. It was he who ended the short tradition that politics were best left in the hands of an aristocracy, and not only encouraged common people to participate in the political process, but convinced many that their own destiny, like his, was linked to taming the Western wilderness.

After the Civil War, the state settled down to growing cotton and never really got back into the mainstream of American life until TVA was established. Today, people who call Nashville the "Wall Street of The South" mean what they say, and the city has gotten so cosmopolitan that many wonder if it still has a legitimate claim to the other title of America's country music capital. And though the blues were developed in Memphis, they're not singing the blues there these days, either. Business is good and getting better. In fact, the whole state is on the move. And the direction is up.

Facing page: the State Capitol in Nashville.

(Facing page) Downtown Memphis from Mud Island. (Above) Newfound
Gap Road in Great Smoky Mountains National Park.

The elegant stern-wheeler *Memphis Queen III* (these pages) glides along the
Mississippi, (above) in Memphis itself, a reminder of a stately, bygone age
when "palaces on paddlewheels" steamed the length of the river.

TEXAS,

Lone Star State

Population (1982): 15,280,000 (3rd)

Size: 267,338 square miles (2nd)

Entered Union: December 29, 1845 (28th)

State Motto: Friendship

State Flower: Bluebonnet

State Bird: Mockingbird

State Tree: Pecan

Industry: petroleum, machinery, electronics, apparel

Agriculture: cattle, cotton, grains, vegetables, citrus, pecans

A few years ago a local Texas television commercial featured a purring young sex kitten selling oil drilling equipment. As if to acknowledge that her audience was limited, she ended her pitch by saying, "If y'all don't have an awl well, git one!"

Well, not everyone in Texas has an oil well, not everyone has a cattle ranch. They're not all millionaires, either. But in Texas, more than any other state, everyone believes they just might – some day. They like entrepreneurs and adventurers in the Lone Star State. They encourage ideas, applaud shows of self-made wealth.

The state has a rich history that goes back to old Mexico and to Stephen Austin, who established the first "Anglo" colony there in 1821. It was the colony that James Bowie, Davy Crockett and others died defending at the Alamo in 1836, and that Sam Houston expanded in battle into an independent republic that lasted, recognized as a full partner by dozens of world powers, for nearly ten years.

It became part of the United States in 1845, but it took a war with Mexico to make statehood really official. And what the United States got for its trouble is something other Americans still can't comprehend. *The Texas Almanac* made an attempt to compare it to the other states: "Texas has in its pine timber belt an area as large as Indiana. Texas has an area along the coast, lying less than 150 feet above sea level, and having a sub-tropical climate, equal to the area of South Carolina. Texas has

an area lying in a middle temperature climate and ranging from 3,000 to 4,000 feet above sea level as large as Pennsylvania. Texas has a mountainous area west of the Pecos as large as West Virginia. Texas has a uniformly good farming country, well-watered and ranging in altitude from 200 to 2,500 feet above sea level, situated in central and midwest parts of the state, equal to the areas of Ohio and Kentucky. Texas has an area on the Edwards Plateau, admirably adapted to cattle, sheep and goat raising and diversified crop production, as large as Tennessee." If it had remained an independent country, it would be bigger than West Germany, Austria, Switzerland, The Netherlands, Denmark and The United Kingdom combined.

It's as diversified as it is big. It still has cowboys and longhorn cattle for them to herd, but it also has more sheep than any other state. It grows more cotton, exports more watermelon and spinach than any other state. It's a leader in banking and construction, electronics and chemicals. It's where America's space program is centered.

Almost nobody doesn't like Texas, even if grudgingly. It has an infectious spirit. But it does have its detractors. Before it was a state, General Sherman said, "If I owned Texas and Hell, I'd rent out Texas and live in Hell." Though the latter is very much an unknown, there is probably an entrepreneur somewhere in Texas right now who would accept that as a very sound business proposition.

Facing page: the fine pink granite Capitol in Austin, the largest capitol in the nation. Overleaf: (left) the Santa Elena Canyon of the Rio Grande, in Big Bend National Park. (Right) the starkly-modern Civic Center in El Paso.

The River Walk (facing page), or *Paseo del Rio*, in San Antonio (above) provides a pleasant stroll both day and night. The legendary Alamo (overleaf, right) still stands in San Antonio, as it did in 1836 when it was defended to the death by an heroic group of Texans against a vastly superior Mexican army. Overleaf: (left) the nearby Mission of San Jose.

Dallas: the Reunion Tower (above) houses a revolving restaurant and cocktail bar, and the Lincoln Hotel (facing page) is one of the most modern in this fast-growing city. Houston (overleaf) counts among its many attractions the Albert Thomas Space Hall of Fame (right, foreground).

The pier (above) lies off Galveston, the main city on Galveston Island, two miles off the Texas coast. Further south along the coast, towards Mexico, stands the town of Corpus Christi, known for its sandy beaches, fine hotels and, above all, its marina (facing page).

UTAH

Beehive State

Population (1982): 1,554,000 (36th)

Size: 84,916 square miles (11th)

Entered Union: January 4, 1896 (45th)

State Motto: Industry

State Flower: Sego lily

State Bird: Seagull

State Tree: Blue spruce

Industry: mining, missiles, electronics, food products

Agriculture: wheat, hay, apples, alfalfa, corn

Americans are proud to point out that their country was founded by people who wanted to escape religious persecution. But all too often, the founding fathers and their offspring practiced persecution themselves. Utah is a living monument to it.

The story began along New York State's Erie Canal in 1827, when a young man named Joseph Smith is said to have had a vision that led to the founding of a new religion known as the Church of Jesus Christ of Latter-day Saints, the Mormon Church.

His followers, driven from place to place, usually violently, finally, in 1847, trekked nearly 1400 miles from Illinois out onto the Great Plains until they reached a spot in the Western desert, stopping when their leader, Brigham Young, declared, "This is the place."

The place he chose to establish the "new Zion" was as hostile as the Negev itself, but the Mormons knew they could make the desert bloom. They were successful, of course, but it was never easy. By 1877, when Brigham Young died, there were 140,000 Mormons in more than 3250 communities working hard at the job.

Discrimination followed them west and their applications for statehood fell on deaf ears in Washington for another two decades before they joined the community of states.

About 75 percent of all Utahns are Mormons today, and the principles of their religion pervade every aspect of life from the state's economy to its government. They believe in hard work, a close-knit family and total abstinence, among other things. The result is that life in Utah isn't quite like life in the other Western states, where individualism is an article of faith. They have the highest birthrate of any state, one of the highest literacy rates and a disposition to stay put that makes its population one of the country's most stable. There is probably less smoking, less drinking, less card-playing done in Utah than any state, East or West.

Utahns are like other Westerners in one respect, their love of the land. Their grandfathers went through such hardship to claim it, the love is only natural. It's a place of desert stillness and mountain beauty. The irrigated greenbelt at the center in the shadow of the Washatch Mountains, the gray desert around the Great Salt Lake, the red and yellow desert in the east, the snow-capped mountains with their sparkling lakes and pine-covered plateaus, are all among the things they love. Until very recent years, the main tourist attraction in Utah was the desire to "see a Mormon." Except to visit the famous and beautiful Tabernacle on Mormon Square in Salt Lake City, the lure is different these days. People go there now to see the strangely beautiful countryside that inspired Brigham Young to say: "This is the place."

Facing page: Bryce Canyon from Paria View, one of the state's most fantastic sights. Overleaf: (left) the untamed beauty of Capitol Reef, seen through the massive span of Hickman Natural Bridge. (Right) Delicate Arch in Arches National Park.

Monumental sandstone rock formations, with names as evocative as the Watchman (facing page) and the Sentinel (above), seen across the waters of the North Fork of the Virgin River, form part of Utah's spectacular Zion Canyon, in Zion National Park.

VERMONT

Green Mountain State

Population (1982): 516,000 (48th)

Size: 9,609 square miles (43rd)

Entered Union: March 4, 1791 (14th)

State Motto: Freedom and Unity

State Flower: Red clover

State Bird: Hermit thrush

State Tree: Sugar maple

Industry: tools, furniture, skis, fishing equipment, computer products

Agriculture: apples, maple sugar, corn, dairy products

One of the toughest trivia questions about the 50 states would be one that asks for the name of the one with the highest rural population. Almost nobody would guess it was Vermont, 66 percent of whose citizens live in rural settings. And it has the country's toughest land use laws that severely restrict ski resorts and shopping malls. Yet it is the 18th most industrialized state.

It is also considered to be one of the most typically "New England" of the New England States, and that makes it all the more attractive to visitors and newcomers. "The qualities of Vermont that were once considered backward are now in vogue," says a state official. "The only reason we have all these lovely old buildings and churches is that nobody had the money to tear them down." "But," adds another, "newcomers pay us the ultimate compliment by trying to imitate us."

It may be that per capita income is lower than in 37 other states, but people migrating there seem to feel that the quality of life in Vermont is a fair tradeoff.

It's a quality of life that hasn't changed much since Colonial times. It has made a typical Vermonter self-reliant, stubborn, independent. They are tolerant and slow to anger, except if someone tries to tell them how to live their lives. And above all, they share a great love for the State of Vermont.

Who can blame them? It's a beautiful place. The three ranges of the Green Mountains come by their name honestly, except in the fall, when their brilliant colors put even the Grand Canyon to shame. There is hardly a barren spot anywhere among its peaks or its notches. The Taconic Mountains along the New York border are gently-rounded and inviting, and form the western boundary of the beautiful Valley of Vermont which merges in the north with the rolling meadows toward the 107-mile-long Lake Champlain. There are more than 400 lakes and ponds in Vermont, and any competition to name the most beautiful of them would surely end up with a hung jury.

Interspersed among it all, the hand of man has created graceful, spired churches and tree-shaded village commons. The countryside is dotted with red barns and pretty white farmhouses, with neatly furrowed fields and peaceful pastures. It has covered bridges and general stores, quaint old inns and a general feeling of travelling back in time to better days.

In spite of an old Vermonter's statement that "A Vermont year is nine months winter and three months of damn poor sleddin'," the climate in Vermont is as delightful as the countryside, though it does get cold in winter, to the delight of skiers up in Killington, Woodstock and other slopes that make it the biggest skiing state east of the Rockies.

Facing page: a sugarhouse, in which sugar and syrup is extracted from maple sap, one of many in the state. Overleaf: (left) a peaceful view of Woodstock. (Right) a ski chair lift near Stowe.

357

Evergreens bring a touch of color to the winter scene (above)
while mist shrouds the Green Mountains (facing page).

SOUTH NORFOLK

HOMER J. BLEVINS
ROBERT E. CLAPP
THOMAS E. COE JR
HOWARD F. COMBS
WAYMAN L. CREGER JR
LARRY B. CREWEY
WILLIAM F. CRUEY JR
CHARLES B. DeBORD JR
SHERMAN T. DINKINS
JAMES B. DIXON
SAMUEL E. DOANE
DANIEL B. DUNSON JR
ROBERT S. DUNTON
JAMES H. EVERHART
GARLAND R. HARRIS
HARRY T. EARLES
GEORGE F. FERGUSON
JAMES H. FLOURNOY
CECIL L. FORD
JOHNNIE B. FREEMAN
THOMAS L. GILLESPIE
FLEMING C. GOOLSBY
JAMES E. GREY

ROBERT L. KEITH
RAYMOND P. LITTLE
JAMES W. McFALL
CLARENCE H. MAIRS
JOHN O. MALOYED
THURMAN H. MARION
LUTHER E. MARTIN JR
PRESTON H. MARTIN JR
WILLIAM S. MERCER JR
MACK H. MOORE
ROBERT H. MOORE
JOHN G. OSBORNE
CHARLES T. PARKS
C. C. PENNINGTON
R. A. PENNINGTON
BLAINE H. PERKINS
EARNEST E. POOLE SR
HOWARD E. POSTON
CHARLES K. POWELL
RICHARD T. PRUITT
LEWIS G. PULLIAM

WILLARD SEVERT
HAROLD C. SHEFFEY
LAWRENCE R. SHORTT
RALEIGH
GLEN D. SHUE
MELVIN C. SHULER SR
ROBERT G. SHUPE
JAMES E. SIMMERMAN
NORMAN B. SMITH
ROBERT J. SOWERS
DAVID H. SPRINKLE
MELVIN E. STUMP
RICHARD O. STURGILL
RAY C. SUTHERLAND
EARL TESTERMAN JR
BALFOUR THOMAS
FRANK R. WALDEN
HENRY T. WARD
GEORGE F. WEST
EMMETT A. WHEELER
JAMES B. WILLIAMS
THOMAS H. WILLIAMS
FRED J. WILSON
JUNIOR J. WOLFE
JAMES W. WOODWARD
HAROLD L. WORLEY
GEORGE A. WRIGHT JR
CHARLES E. WYATT

GEORGE W. KISER
FRANCIS C. KITE
KNIGHTEN
KNUPP
KNUPP JR
ANDREW J. LAW JR
H. LAM
LAMBERT
LEAP
LEE
McDANIE
DONALDSON
MILLER
BENJAMIN A. MYERS
R. MYERS
NEFF
FRANCIS H. PAINTER
A. PIRKEY
REYNOLDS
C. RHODES
D. RIGGLEMAN
GEORGE W. ROACH
M. SHANK
G. SHERMAN

VIRGINIA

Old Dominion

Population (1982): 5,491,000 (13th)

Size: 40,817 square miles (36th)

Entered Union: June 26, 1788 (10th)

State Motto: Sic Semper Tyrannis (Thus Always to Tyrants)

State Flower: Dogwood

State Bird: Cardinal

State Tree: Dogwood

Industry: textiles, apparel, food processing, shipbuilding, chemicals

Agriculture: tobacco, soybeans, peanuts, corn

It's the state that gave us George Washington and Thomas Jefferson, George Mason and James Madison. It gave America its first aristocracy in the families who established plantations in its Tidewater country and ruled the surrounding countryside like English lords. It also gave America its vision of human rights.

Virginia still holds fast to her roots, but its a fast-changing place with thriving industry on land that once was completely dependent on the tobacco crop and in cities growing by leaps and bounds surrounded by even faster-growing suburbs.

Yet it manages to maintain the rural character that has attracted newcomers since Pennsylvania Germans began wandering down into the Shenandoah Valley in the 18th century.

There are all kinds of beauty in Virginia. It begins with the coastal plain they call "Tidewater," a belt about 100 miles wide from the Atlantic Ocean and the Chesapeake Bay. Its bays and tidal rivers and the rich farmland around them were the natural setting for the first settlements and the reason why British merchants were so anxious to invest so much in the idea of colonizing North America.

As the colonizers went westward, they found the gently rolling country of the Piedmont, the foothills of the Blue Ridge Mountains, which rise abruptly to more than 4000 feet in many places. The valleys to the west of the Blue Ridge, together known as The Valley of Virginia, make up some of the most beautiful countryside in any of the Eastern states.

Though the American Revolution was fought largely in the north, it came to Virginia in the spring of 1779, when a British fleet sailed into Hampton Roads and attempted to set up a blockade. The attempt failed, but it established a British presence that came to a head in 1781, when they dispatched a small force of men to capture Thomas Jefferson and the Virginia legislature. The army, entrenched at Portsmouth and Yorktown, were also on the trail of a force of Americans serving under the Marquis de Lafayette. They met at Yorktown, where a French fleet had set up a blockade that prevented any reinforcements from arriving. After a three-week siege, the British General Cornwallis surrendered to the Virginian George Washington and America was finally free to go her own way.

The American Civil War ended in Virginia, too, when another Virginian, Robert E. Lee, surrendered at Appomattox in 1865. The war itself was fought more on Virginia soil than in any other state, putting places like Hampton Roads, Manassas, Spotsylvania and Richmond forever in American history.

It took nearly 100 years for Virginia to recover completely from the effects of that war. In 1940, the official guidebook, compiled by the Federal Writers' Project, said: "... the elders seldom talk fifteen minutes without some reference to the War Between the States." The talk is along different lines these days. But Virginians are aware of their past, all of it. They know how much the nation owes to it.

Facing page: the Virginia War Memorial, Richmond. Overleaf: (left) George Washington's home at Mount Vernon, on a hill above the Potomac. (Right) the Great Hall of the George Washington Masonic National Memorial, in Alexandria.

Facing page: one of the numerous fine buildings at the University of Virginia, Charlottesville. Above: Monticello, home of Thomas Jefferson, was begun in 1769 and is regarded as a classic example of American architecture.

Many fine and historic houses have been restored in Williamsburg (above) to recreate and preserve the atmosphere of its 18th-century capital role. Facing page: the rebuilt Governor's Palace on Palace Green. Overleaf: (left) one of Virginia's popular resorts. (Right) the New Cape Henry Lighthouse, the tallest cast-iron lighthouse in the United States.

WASHINGTON

Evergreen State

Population (1982): 4,245,000 (20th)

Size: 68,192 square miles (20th)

Entered Union: November 11, 1889 (42nd)

State Motto: Alki (By and By)

State Flower: Rhododendron

State Bird: Goldfinch

State Tree: Hemlock

Industry: aircraft, pulp and paper, lumber, plywood, processed foods

Agriculture: apples, wheat, potatoes, hay

The history of exploration of the American continent revolves around the search for a Northwest Passage, a convenient water route from the Atlantic to the Pacific and the fabled Orient.

Many thought they found it in the form of Washington's Columbia River, but others knew they had found something better: a beautiful place to live in the Northwest corner of the United States.

Though Washington is the place most of the world's airlines get their big jets from, the typical vision of most Americans is a place where Indians still roam the woods. They're wrong about the Indians, of course, but there are still plenty of virgin forests for anyone to roam thrugh. There are mountains to climb, too, and streams to fish, lakes to enjoy and a seacoast to take your breath away.

There is also prairie country east of the Cascade Mountains, and former deserts that have been made to bloom.

People have been going there to live since 1792, when Captain George Vancouver sailed into Puget Sound and wrote rhapsodies about Mount Rainier. Fifty years later, life got tough for beavers and otters when the trappers established themselves there. Lumbermen arrived next, determined, it seemed, to clear as much of the forest as hard work would allow. In the mid-1850s a gold rush brought even more adventurers, but most of them went off to Alaska in search of even more. Seattle was

their gateway, though, and much of the gold they managed to find found its way into the United States through that gateway.

Though the average rainfall in Eastern Washington is less than ten inches a year, the Olympic Peninsula, with an average upwards of 130 inches, takes the prize as the wettest place on the entire continent. But that doesn't stop people from settling in the western part of the state, where more than three quarters of the population lives. If the sun doesn't shine all that much, they live there because it's so dazzlingly beautiful.

The shoreline of Puget Sound zigzags for 1800 miles and many of those miles are lined with lush forests. The mountainsides give dramatic vistas, the Sound itself gives a waterscape dotted with hundreds of islands, many of which are charming places to live. And there are plenty of people responding to the lure. In spite of the fact that only San Francisco has a higher rate of suicide and alcoholism than Seattle, which also has the country's record for divorce, the population of Washington grew by an astounding 25 percent in the 1970s.

But still, though cosmopolitan in its cities, Washington maintains the qualities that gave it its nickname, "The Evergreen State." It's green, and seems destined to stay that way forever. But it is also the pink of rhododendron, the blues, yellows and reds of wildflowers, the white of snowcapped mountains and glaciers.

Facing page and overleaf, left: the Space Needle in Seattle, largest city in Washington. Overleaf: (right) Great Bend on the Hood Canal.

The Palouse River has carved the yawning chasm (above) on its way to join the Snake River. Facing page: Takhlakh Lake reflects the slopes of Mt. Adams. Overleaf: (left) the summit of Glacier Peak dominates the Cascade Mountains. (Right) Mount St. Helens before the eruption of May 18, 1980.

Mount Shuksan (these pages) in the far north of the state, within
the boundaries of North Cascades National Park, is near the
important skiing center of Mount Baker.

WEST VIRGINIA

Mountain State

Population (1982): 1,948,000 (34th)

Size: 24,181 square miles (41st)

Entered Union: June 20, 1863 (35th)

State Motto: Montani Semper Liberi (Mountaineers Are Always Free)

State Flower: Rhododendron

State Bird: Cardinal

State Tree: Sugar maple

Industry: mining, machinery, plastics, hardwood products, glass timber

Agriculture: apples, peaches, tobacco, corn, wheat

Of all the great American folk heroes, one that modern man relates best to is John Henry, the "steel-drivin' man" who took a twenty-pound hammer and bested a steamd-driven machine. The story, told in rhyme, says: "The men that made that steam drill Thought it was mighty fine; John Henry drove his fourteen feet While the steam drill only made nine."

John Henry was a West Virginian. The contest purportedly took place in 1872, when the Chesapeake and Ohio Railroad cut the Big Bend Tunnel in the southeastern part of the state.

It isn't far from there to White Sulphur Springs and the famous Greenbriar Hotel, which has been one of the country's poshest resorts since Colonial days, and was even the summer residence of presidents in the first half of the 19th century.

The sanctity of hard work, the pampering of the rich are just two of the contrasts that make West Virginia such a fascinating place. Even the landscape is diverse. It is a land of high mountains (it is the most mountainous of all of the 50 states), wide valleys and narrow gorges. There are deep forests and open fields, modern cities and hundreds of "company towns" built to serve the state's major industry: coal mining.

Well over 100 million tons of coal are taken from the West Virginia hills every year, making mining far and away the state's major industry. Many feel it is West Virginia's only industry.

There are others, of course. The state produces natural gas and has a strong chemical industry. West Virginia glass is the finest produced in the United States. It ranks among the top five states in minerals.

Yet West Virginians are, by and large, poor. It is the heartland of "Appalachia," a place that estimates it loses some 75 percent of its young people as soon as they finish school.

There is very little immigration from other states, which makes West Virginia one of the few whose population is almost entirely native-born. It makes the family reunion a lasting West Virginia institution. Most of the family members who go home for them go from places like Ohio and Florida or from Detroit and Chicago, cities which have established neighborhoods composed entirely of former West Virginians.

The state itself is a former part of Virginia. From its earliest days, people in Eastern and Western Virginia were sharply divided on the issue of slavery, and the division became a wide gulf when John Brown was hanged for seizing the Federal arsenal at Harper's Ferry in 1859. When war broke out and Virginia seceded from the Union, the western counties voted to form a new state that would be loyal to the Northern cause. A popular vote was held and statehood was approved by a vote of 18,862 to 514. In the face of that kind of popularity, President Lincoln signed a proclamation giving them statehood on April 20, 1863. Ninety days later it became the 35th of the United States.

Facing page: the bridge at Harpers Ferry.

Facing page: the town of Harpers Ferry. In October 1859 John Brown, as part of
his plan to free slaves, seized the town's arsenal (above) and remained
barricaded inside until defeated and ultimately executed by Federal authorities.

WISCONSIN

Badger State

Population (1982): 4,765,000 (16th)

Size: 56,154 square miles (26th)

Entered Union: May 29, 1848 (30th)

State Motto: Forward

State Flower: Violet

State Bird: Robin

State Tree: Sugar maple

Industry: machinery, food processing, metal products, paper products, wood products

Agriculture: corn, beans, oats, cranberries, peas, beets

Before World War II, slightly more than half the total population of Wisconsin was either born in a foreign country or had parents who were. More than 40 percent of those came from Germany.

That's one very good reason why Milwaukee was once America's beer capital and why one beer company's slogan for many years was, "I'm from Milwaukee and I ought to know." On the other hand, one of its competitors told the world that its beer came from "the land of the sky-blue waters."

Wisconsin is set between Lakes Michigan and Superior and 500 miles of its borders are lake shore. But it also has some 4000 major lakes scattered within its borders, not to mention nearly 5000 bodies of waters more appropriately called ponds.

The brewers aren't as important in Milwaukee as they once were. Even Schlitz, "the beer that made Milwaukee famous," isn't made there any longer. But the city still has more bowling alleys and neighborhood bars than most other cities, and a friendly glass of beer makes one of their famous cold winter nights a little easier to endure.

But if you should order a glass of milk in a Wisconsin bar, patrons are just as likely to stand up and cheer as laugh up their sleeves. There are nearly two million cows in Wisconsin, more than twice the human population of Milwaukee and Madison combined. In fact there are more dairy cows in Wisconsin than in any other state. They produce some 40 percent of all the cheese made in the United States, including Colby, a type that was invented in Wisconsin. The town that gave it its name was originally settled by a dozen families who hid themselves in the woods to escape the Civil War draft and weren't discovered until the war was over and a road was built through their forest.

At that time, Wisconsin was one of the country's major wheat-producing states, but soil exhaustion and better wheat fields in the Dakotas and Minnesota made the industry marginal at best.

It was a newspaperman in Fort Atkinson, William Dempster Hoard, who showed them the way to go. He expanded a dairy column in his weekly paper to a full page, then a separate section. By 1872, his paper didn't carry news of anything but dairy farming. But by then the Scandinavian and German farmers had gotten the message. Dairying was harder than wheat farming, but hard work never bothered them in the first place.

There are more than 450,000 acres of virgin wilderness in Wisconsin, the North Woods. It's a territory that looks very much like it did when French trappers waded through its streams more than two centuries ago. In the last half of the 20th century it seems to have suddenly been discovered by people who like living close to nature. It's the fastest-growing part of the state and with that growth is coming a lesson for the future for other states. Many of the North Woods newcomers earn their living at home using computers connected to mainframes in other parts of the country.

Facing page: the interior of the State Capitol in Madison. Overleaf: (left) the Wolf River at Markton. (Right) Lake Geneva.

Above: wild lupins near Washburn. Facing page: one of the many picturesque farms north of Chippewa Falls. Overleaf: (left) the Wisconsin River at Wisconsin Dells. (Right) the view from Point Lookout, Wyalusing State Park.

WYOMING

Equality State

Population (1982): 502,000 (49th)

Size: 97,914 square miles (9th)

Entered Union: July 10, 1890 (44th)

State Motto: Equal Rights

State Flower: Indian paintbrush

State Bird: Meadowlark

State Tree: Cottonwood

Industry: petroleum, coal, wood products

Agriculture: cattle and sheep, wheat, beans, hay

When you drive into Wyoming, the signs that welcome you include a silhouette of a cowboy on a bucking bronco. If you should miss it, the same symbol is repeated on the license plates of every vehicle and chances are good that if you stop at a motel, the cowboy will stand out on everything from the breakfast menu to the final bill.

The message, of course, is that Wyoming is cowboy country. But as you drive through its plains and valleys and over its mountains, you don't need symbolism. It's all around you.

An early guidebook said that "Wyoming is a place where you can look farther and see less than any other place in the world." It went on to say, "although Wyoming is a land of great distances, the various sections of the state are not isolated. A network of oiled highways makes it possible to travel from one corner of the state to the other in less than a day's time. Few of the settlements of 100 or more population are more than ten miles' drive from an oiled highway." That was 50 years ago, when an "oiled highway" was a dirt road with oil on it and the last ten miles to a settlement was a dusty, rutted path not much wider than a Model A Ford.

Things have changed, of course. There is coal under those cattle ranges. There is oil and gas, too, and uranium. It's resulting in a population boom of sorts. By the time of the 1982 census, there were 5.2 people per square mile in Wyoming and some old-timers were talking about going up to Alaska for a little elbow room.

They're not serious, of course. Everything they want out of life is in Wyoming, and for the right kind of person there is no better life. Most Wyomingites keep a hunting rifle and a fishing pole in their pickup trucks. And though they prize their solitude, they love sharing it, which is one reason why tourism is a major Wyoming industry. The other, of course, is Wyoming itself. It's the home of the spectacular Bighorn Mountains, of Yellowstone National Park, of Jackson Hole and the indescribable Grand Tetons.

At first glance, Wyoming's image is of a man's world. Life isn't easy there. But it was the first of all the states to take equal rights seriously and women were given the right to vote when it was still a territory. In 1870 it had America's first female justice of the peace in South Pass City, as wild a mining town as the West has produced. In 1925 Wyoming became the first state in the Union to have a woman governor.

In 1844, Daniel Webster said that Wyoming was "a region of savages, wild beasts, shifting sands, whirlwinds of dust and prairie dogs." Someone just passing through might say he was right. But someone like that can just keep right on going. Wyoming doesn't appeal to everyone, but its appeal is something very special.

Facing page: the snow-covered Grand Tetons. Overleaf: (left) the spouting Castle Geyser and (right) Morning Glory Pool, both in Yellowstone National Park. Following pages: Yellowstone National Park.

List of Illustrations